What a gift this author has for ⌐
complex truths accessible! With
conversational style, Francine is skilled in proposing
questions which draw her readers to engage thoughtfully and
emotionally on a wide range of aspects of the Christian faith.

In this book, Francine handles challenging topics like
wisdom, trust, trials, and justice with apparent ease and with
faith-strengthening clarity and urgency.

Whilst she clearly teaches us out of her wealth of life
experience and contemporary examples, she does not base
her discussions on her own authority or personal insight.
Rather, she grounds every one of her 20 stimulating chapters
in the authority of Scripture, as the guiding word of God. She
leads her readers by the hand through relevant passages from
the Bible, explaining and applying each idea as she goes.

Francine has a wide readership in mind with this book. If
you have been a Christian for many years, you will find
something to stretch and refresh your walk with the Lord.
And if you would not call yourself a Christian or are looking
at the teachings of the Bible for the first time, you will be
gently, yet passionately, invited to see what wonderful and
life-changing things are on offer to those who get to know
God through Jesus. Whatever stage you're at, this book has
been written to build every woman up in her faith, making it
the perfect resource for private reflection, group study or to
share with a friend.

*Sally Gobbett, wife of the senior pastor at Highfields
Church, Cardiff.*

Whispers of Love

Whispers of Love

A collection of Christian talks to
challenge and encourage women

FRANCINE LOOSE

First published 2021 by Francine Loose using Kindle Direct Publishing.

ISBN 9798542480930

2021 09 23

Acknowledgements

I would like to express my indebtedness to Mrs Joan Smith of Abergavenny, whose original suggestion led to the writing of this book.

I am extremely grateful to Ms Rachel Smith (no relation to Joan Smith) for giving of her time to proof-read the text and making many amendments.

Also, I would like to thank Rachel for her thoughtful and appropriate art work which has added a further dimension to the book.

And last, but certainly not least, my heartfelt thanks to my husband, Andrew, for his encouragement, support and, in particular, his IT skills and expertise which have been vital in bringing this work to publication.

Soli Deo Gloria

Contents

Foreword

Spring 2020. The nation was in national lockdown, due to the coronavirus pandemic.

Churches were now closed. For many years, I have had the privilege of serving the Lord in speaking at women's meetings in a number of churches. This was no longer possible. Bookings had been cancelled and I had no further engagements in the diary as no one knew when these meetings would start up again.

I was speaking to a very dear Christian friend on the phone. I expressed my sadness that this area of service was no longer possible and would not recommence for some considerable time.

The friend, without a moment's hesitation, told me she felt I should consider putting into print the talks I had given through the years, as a way of encouraging others and as a way of reaching a wider audience with the word of God, which He had laid on my heart during many years of ministry to women.

I initially put the idea to the back of my mind. It was not something I had ever previously considered doing. During the late spring and summer, I pursued outside activities like walking and meeting friends in the garden when restrictions allowed. I also took up painting and spent time chatting to folk on the phone.

But in late September, we were put back into local lockdown. Now we were in autumn and heading to winter. The prospect of many hours indoors as the weather became cooler and wetter was daunting.

Then the conversation with my friend came back to me.

And so, this book was written.

My prayer and hope is that those who read it will be blessed, encouraged, taught and challenged by what they read and will grow in their daily walk with God.

And most of all, that the Lord Himself will receive all the praise and glory due to His name.

Francine Loose

1

Testimony

I haven't always been a Christian. I wasn't born a Christian nor was I brought up in a Christian home. Before becoming a Christian, I lived a life centred on me. I had goals for my life which concerned my desires, my interests and pleasures. I had it all planned out with no thought for God at all.

My parents, though not Christian, were what would have been described in those days as highly principled and God fearing. They sent me to Sunday school and in my mid-teens I started to attend the local Methodist Church. I loved singing and at that time I had a lovely singing voice. It was not long before I was asked to join the choir. So, I became a church attender but still lived for myself. I had no idea how my sin offended a holy God or what He had done for me through His Son, Jesus.

A few weeks before my 19th birthday, I moved away from home to go to university. While back at home for the Christmas holiday, my mother was suddenly taken ill in the middle of the night and died before help could reach her.

It was during the months following her death that I became aware of God working in my life. Really, it was from the day of her funeral, when I remember being given a peace which passes all understanding, learning later that it was a peace that comes only from God.

On my return to university, God continued to work in my life. He used friends who were Christian to support and help me through those days of grief and bereavement. He kept His hand on me. And little by little He used these friends to draw me closer to Him.

In time, they invited me to the University Christian Union meetings. It was here that I heard for the first time the Gospel of the Lord Jesus Christ.

I heard how we are all born as sinners. Paul, writing to the early church in Rome, says very clearly:

..... all have sinned and fall short of the glory of God.[1]

I heard how that sin comes between us and a holy God. To my amazement, I learnt about God's love for us and how He had a rescue plan to save us from sin. You see, He sent Jesus, His own Son from the splendour of Heaven to die on this earth in our place. I discovered when listening to the many men of God who spoke each week at those Christian Union meetings that Jesus, the sinless one died for me that I may know forgiveness for my sins and know peace with God the Father. And how He rose from the dead to overcome death, to give me and all who call on His name the gift of eternal life.

Over some months, God took away the scales from my eyes and spoke to me personally through the Scriptures and through the messages from the speakers who addressed us week by week. And so, by His grace and mercy, I was able to receive Jesus as my Saviour and gave my life to Him.

How did things change after that?

I now wanted to know Jesus in a deeper way. I started to read my Bible. I started to talk to God in prayer and saw answers come. I attended the local church in the town as well as becoming fully involved in the work of the Christian Union. You see, I was learning that Jesus was not only my Saviour who had rescued me from the pit of sin but was also my Lord. I needed to learn how He wanted me to live. I was no longer following the plans I mentioned earlier but following the plan God had for my life.

Romans chapter 8 has been very important and precious to me – it begins:

> *Therefore, there is now no condemnation for those who are in Christ Jesus.*

And later on, in the same chapter we read,

> *For I am convinced that neither death nor life, neither angels nor demons, neither the present nor the future, nor any powers, neither height nor depth, nor anything else in all*

---

[1] Romans 3:23

creation, will be able to separate us from the love of God that is in Christ Jesus our Lord.[2]

I no longer wanted to live a life pleasing myself but wanted to please God and serve Him in whatever way I could.

All this happened around 50 years ago. As you would expect, a lot of water has gone under the bridge in that time. There have been many blessings and also trials and difficulties along the journey of life. But God has been with me throughout, leading, guiding and guarding.

In particular, I can testify to the truth of an Old Testament verse which says,

Through the Lord's mercy we are not consumed, because His compassions fail not. They are new every morning. Great is your faithfulness.[3]

These words have been written as a hymn which was sung at our wedding in 1973. The God who revealed Himself to me has been faithful over these many years.

I praise Him and thank Him for all that He is and all He has done in Jesus.

Can I ask if you have given any thought to such matters in your own life? It is vitally important that you do so, before it is too late.

---

[2] Romans 8:38-39
[3] Lamentations 3:22-23, NKJV

2

"Name above all names"

In commerce and business, marketing bosses know the importance of the name of a product they are trying to sell. For example, do you remember the cleaning product Jif, that thick creamy substance that cleaned all manner of surfaces?

In 2001, Unilever decided it was time to change its name, now calling it Cif. Apparently, the company wanted to market the product across Europe and wanted to standardise the name across all the European nations. Many European languages didn't pronounce the hard J as in Jif, so it was changed to Cif so that everyone throughout the continent would be able to pronounce it without difficulty.

I wonder, does anyone have a particularly unusual name? My own name, I guess, is quite unusual. "Francine". It was actually given as my middle name, but an uncle liked it better than my given first name and called me by it from almost the day of my birth. It seems everyone else followed suit and that is what I have always been known as. I guess the plus side of an unusual name is that people don't tend to forget it!

Have you noticed how nowadays new babies, often those born to so called celebrities, are often given names which we might regard as not just unusual but very different from what we would have known as children's names in the past?

Let me give a few examples by way of illustration. We have Fifi Trixibelle; Moon Unit; Apple; Audio; Birdie; Blue Ivy; Bronx; Cricket; Denim; Future; North, -----child of Kanye whose surname is West, so the child's name is North West.

And Jamie Oliver, the renowned chef and restauranteur has five children named Buddy Bear, Petal Blossom, Poppy Honey, Daisy Boo and River Rocket.

Do names actually mean anything?

Historically, the name of a new-born child was chosen because of its meaning. I know when my own two children were born my husband and I looked at the meaning of the names we liked before making a final decision. You can buy books of baby names, giving the meaning of each one or even go on the internet and google vast lists of names and their meanings in no time at all.

But, you know, if we go back to Bible times, the meaning of a name was very important, far more important than it has been in recent generations or is today. Even if the meaning of the name is considered when being chosen it is rarely if ever referred to again. However this was not the case in Bible times, when great significance was placed on the choice of name.

Let's look at a few examples to illustrate what I mean.

First of all, the name Moses:

This name is a Hebrew word meaning "drawn out of the water" which of course you may remember is exactly what happened to him, for as a small child he was rescued from the bulrushes by the Pharaoh's daughter.

Next there is Abraham:

This name means "father of many". Again, this is reflecting what he was to become as he did become just that, the father of the nation of Israel as the Lord had promised to him.

Then we have Ruth:

This means "friend" and those of you who know the story of Ruth will remember she was just that in a very real way to her mother- in-law, Naomi.

And the name Naomi itself means "pleasantness" When her life was no longer pleasant, but hard and difficult following the death of her husband and two sons, and while living in a foreign land, she changed her name to Mara, which means "bitter".

Perhaps by now, you are beginning to see the importance of names and their meaning when used in the Scriptures.

In the New Testament, we can think of the story of John the Baptist. Those familiar with the story will remember that the name John was divinely given to him by an angel before his birth.

Zechariah, John's father, was a priest at the time of King Herod. His mother, Elizabeth, was a descendent of Aaron. They were both

8

godly people. But they had no children. And they were getting on a bit. They were old.

Clearly, when we read the account of the story in Luke's gospel, we know that Zechariah had been praying for a child. But it is also clear that Zechariah didn't expect things to turn out as they did. For an angel of the Lord came to him and told him that his wife would give birth to a son and that Zechariah was to call him John.

Zechariah was full of doubts and unbelief. He told the angel he was an old man and his wife was also very old.

And you may remember the angel Gabriel telling him that because he did not believe, he would be struck dumb until the birth of the child. This is exactly what happened. Zechariah could not speak.

Some months later, Elizabeth became pregnant as foretold and, in the fulness of time, the baby was born.

Now in those days it would have been the custom to name a son after his father. But Elizabeth spoke up and said his name was to be John. The relatives wondered why that name had been chosen as there was no one called John in their family. So, they signalled to Zechariah to find out what he wanted the child to be called. He wrote on a writing tablet, "His name is John". Immediately he was able to speak once more.

Everyone wondered what this child would become, for they declared, "The Lord's hand was with him".

So, we see here a great significance being placed in the name, a name divinely given to this particular child. And of course, as we read on in the Gospel, we know that John was the one who prepared the way for the coming of Christ and the one who baptised Him.

This now brings us to the **Name of Jesus, the Name above all names**.

The following Bible passage, recording details of the birth of Jesus, is from Matthew's Gospel:

[18] This is how the birth of Jesus Christ came about: His mother Mary was pledged to be married to Joseph, but before they came together, she was found to be with child through the Holy Spirit. [19] Because Joseph her husband was a righteous man and did not want to expose her to public disgrace, he had in mind to divorce her quietly.

9

20 But after he had considered this, an angel of the Lord appeared to him in a dream and said, "Joseph son of David, do not be afraid to take Mary home as your wife, because what is conceived in her is from the Holy Spirit. 21 She will give birth to a son, and you are to give him the name Jesus, because he will save his people from their sins."4

I want to draw your attention in this passage to two very important points.

Firstly, Mary and Joseph didn't choose the name for the baby she was carrying. This baby was no ordinary baby, He was the Son of God and so His name was decreed by God and told by the angel sent from God. The name was to be Jesus. Many names could have been chosen. Why this particular one?

It's all down to the second point, the meaning of the name. As we have already said, this was of great significance and importance.

These verses tell us that He, that is Jesus, will save His people from their sins. So straight away we are told, through the name given to Him before His birth, why He came and why He was to be known primarily by this name, Jesus. He came as Saviour. This is why He came. The name Jesus means "The Lord saves". This was His mission and His purpose in coming to live on earth amongst men and women.

People often speak of Jesus as having been a good man, or a healer of the sick or a worker of other miracles. All these things may well be true of Him, but we mustn't miss the reason He left His Heavenly Father and the Heavenly place. And we know what that is from the name. He came to be Saviour. His purpose in coming is clearly expressed in His Name. This Name Jesus is above all other names.

There are of course many names in Scripture by which Jesus is known. Matthew continues his record in this way:

22 All this took place to fulfil what the Lord had said through the prophet: 23 "The virgin will be with child and will give birth to a son, and they will call him Immanuel"—which means, "God with us."

---

4 Matthew 1:18-21

Here we are told that Jesus will be called Immanuel, which means God with us. This is another name of huge significance for now we know without a shadow of doubt who this baby is. He is God. The verse is clear. There can be no doubt. He is God in human flesh, in the form of a human, in a human body.

We can also turn back to the Old Testament where the writers were looking forward to the coming of Messiah.

The prophet to whom Matthew refers is Isaiah who recorded what the Lord had said about Messiah:

For to us a child is born,
to us a son is given,
and the government will be on his shoulders.
And he will be called
Wonderful Counsellor, Mighty God,
Everlasting Father, Prince of Peace.[5]

Elsewhere He is known as King or King of Kings, Lord, Logos – meaning the Word, Son of God, Son of Man, Master, Son of David, Lamb of God, Second Adam and Last Adam, the Christ.

All these names tell us something about Jesus and who He is. But the name He was given at birth is the most significant of all as it tells us He came as Saviour. It speaks of His work of redemption on earth and is like no other name.

If we look in the New Testament letters, we find there an emphasis on the name of Jesus.

For example, Paul in the letter to the church at Philippi says,

Therefore, God exalted Him, (that is Jesus), to the highest
place and gave Him the name that is above every name, ...[6]

This brings us to the crux of what this chapter is all about: the **name that is above every other name**.

For then Paul goes on,

*..... that at the **name** of Jesus, every knee should bow, in*
heaven and on earth and under the earth, and every tongue
confess that Jesus Christ is Lord, to the glory of God the
Father.[7]

[5] Isaiah 9:6
[6] Philippians 2:9
[7] Philippians 2:10-11

The verse doesn't say that everyone will bow at the sight of Jesus or at the voice of Jesus. No. **At the name of Jesus.**

Do you see how significant that name is? It almost feels like we're on holy ground here.

Jesus Himself stresses His own name, this time when speaking of prayer.

In John's Gospel, Jesus tells us when we pray to pray in His name. He tells us the Father will answer the prayers that we ask in Jesus' name.

Jesus, Name above all names. It's a wonderful name. At least it is to some, but not to all. Why do I say that?

To answer that question, I want to consider three Ps, three words beginning with the letter P which will describe how this name is viewed and used by all people. Everyone falls into one category or another. As you read on, consider carefully which category you come into.

The first P is the word **profaned.**

The name Jesus or more usually Jesus Christ is profaned by many people. They have no interest in the name or the person, yet they use His name as a swear word. It is used as a curse. Some people use it quite a lot. They take the name of Jesus in vain, blasphemously. Such people are irreligious as they have no interest in the things of God at all and just use the name of Jesus as a profanity.

And sadly, there are religious people who quote the right things, who go through religious ritual and ceremony but for whom there has been no change of life, no change of heart. They too profane the name of Jesus and take it in vain.

The second P is the word **peripheral.**

Peripheral. On the edge, on the fringe of things.

People who fall into this category keep Jesus on the edge of their life, on the fringe. He is peripheral, not central. So, they are happy to think of having Him included, shall we say, at a funeral, or a baby's christening or at Christmas time when they sing carols and perhaps attend a Christmas service in church. But for most of the time they are too busy to be bothered with Him at all and to a large extent live their life as though He doesn't exist. Jesus is on the peripheral but not central.

The third P is the word **precious.**

To others the name Jesus is a precious name. Why is that?

The name Jesus is precious to those who have seen that they are sinners and have come to believe in Jesus as their Saviour, the one who saves them from their sin. The Bible makes it clear that there is no other way by which we can be saved.

The apostle Peter, when arrested by the Jewish rulers, elders and teachers of the law, told them very clearly who this Jesus really was. He told them:

> *Salvation is found in no-one else, for there is no other name under heaven given to men by which we must be saved.*[8]

Can I ask you a very personal question? What does the name of Jesus mean to you?

Is it a name you use as a profanity?

Is it a name that is on the peripheral of your life?

Or is it precious to you?

God works in our hearts. He sent Jesus to be the answer to the problem of sin.

We must acknowledge our sin and then we must put our trust in this Saviour, Jesus, and serve Him as Lord of our life.

Jesus Christ has been given the name above all names, the highest seat of honour, the right to reign and rule in our lives.

Yet so often the busyness of our lives and the diversions of this world distract us from knowing the most important person we could ever know.

After the utter humiliation of death on the cross, Jesus was exalted to the highest place and given the name that is above every name, Lord and Saviour.

Now we need to look carefully again at what Paul goes on to say in those verses already quoted from his letter to the church in Philippi:

> *[10] that at the name of Jesus every knee should bow,*
> *in heaven and on earth and under the earth,*
> *[11] and every tongue confess that Jesus Christ is Lord,*
> *to the glory of God the Father.*

---

[8] Acts 4:12

13

Every knee will bow at the name of Jesus. This means those who have profaned and those who are still profaning the name of Jesus, and all those who treat His name with hatred and total disgust will bow to that very name that they have so misused in this way.

Whatever office they may have held in this life, however famous or insignificant, however rich or poor, it makes no difference.

And the same applies to everyone reading this book. All, believer and unbeliever alike, will bow to Him and to His name.

But Paul goes further – not only will every one bow before Jesus Christ as Lord but they will actually recognise the Lordship of Jesus Christ:

..... and every tongue confess that Jesus Christ is Lord, ...

So, what do we see here?

The same tongue that has blasphemed, that has used the name of Jesus as a curse, as a swear word, will now confess who He is.

No swear word now. No peripheral use of the name now. No, a confession that He is Lord, Lord of Lords and King of Kings.

Paul is referring here to that great day on which the whole world will be judged. He is speaking about those who are in Heaven at the time of Jesus' triumphant return; those who are alive, (both believers and those who refuse to accept the way of salvation) and those who have died without knowing Christ as their Saviour.

Everyone will bow and confess that He is Lord when Jesus comes again.

Some, of course, will do it willingly because they know Jesus as their personal Saviour and so love to confess His name.

However, those who did not or do not know Him as their Saviour and Lord will do so unwillingly. They will have no choice in the matter. There will be no alternative, for on that day, the day of grace will have ended. On that day, there will be no opportunity to repent and come to faith.

The Bible tells us that **now** is the time to recognise that we are all sinners, to repent of our sin and put our trust in the Lord Jesus Christ.

And if we do put our trust in Jesus, that One whose Name is above all other names, that Name will be truly precious to each one of us.

So, what is in a name? When you think about it, it doesn't really matter what we think of the name Cif or whether we prefer Jif; nor does it matter what Kanye West or Jamie Oliver name their children.

But the name Jesus and what we think of that? Now that really does matter.

3

Are you ready for Christmas?

"Are you ready for Christmas?"

I expect you are asked that question many times in the weeks running up to Christmas.

What exactly do people mean when they ask that question?

Well, of course they are thinking about all the numerous things that have to be got ready for enjoying Christmas; all that has to be done in time for what they see as the Big Day. Everyone is rushing about, stressed, tired, anxious lest they are **not ready** for this very important day. Life is super frantic, much more hectic than normal.

Perhaps you have been asked some of these questions.

"Have you ordered the turkey yet?"

"Have you made your Christmas cake and pudding?"

"Have you baked enough mince pies?"

"Have you finished the Christmas shopping, wrapped the presents, written the cards, and decorated the house?"

So much at this time of year is about money, about pleasure, about enjoying ourselves. There are festivities to take part in, Christmas parties and school plays to attend.

Have you made the right costume for the concert or bought the right dress for the office party?

Have you got everything ready when visitors call or come to stay?

Oh yes, we certainly ask the question, "Are we ready for Christmas?"

What is Christmas about anyway?

Consider the words of this little rhyme,

It came without ribbons
It came without tags
It came without packages, boxes or bags.
Maybe Christmas doesn't come from a store.
Maybe Christmas means something far more.

17

According to research, Christmas is life's sixth most stressful event, coming behind divorce, moving to a new house and changing jobs.

In a survey carried out by the UK's largest online gift giving company, 17 out of 20 people find buying gifts difficult, 13 out of 20 find shopping stressful, 12 out of 20 worry that people won't like what they have bought for them and a similar number have had the awful experience of seeing the disappointment on the face of someone when they opened their gift!

Another study has shown that January 8th is the busiest day of the year for divorce lawyers after the pressures of Christmas.

A survey done to find out the views of people concerning Christmas found that only 10% of adults thought that its religious meaning is the most important thing about Christmas.

So, what is Christmas really all about?

As well as being caught up in the commercialised side of Christmas it is easy to get caught up in the sentimental side of Christmas. We think perhaps of the baby in the manger, the sheep and shepherds on the hillside, the plight of Mary and Joseph with nowhere to stay when the baby is due to be born, without having any idea, any understanding of what Christmas is really about or what it really means.

There was a Marks and Spencer advert one Christmas which went something like this:

> Christmas wouldn't be Christmas without mince pies.
> Christmas wouldn't be Christmas without silk lingerie.
> Christmas wouldn't be Christmas without Christmas decorations.
> Christmas wouldn't be Christmas without Marks and Spencer.

Perhaps you agree with that sentiment or would prefer to add some essentials of your own.

But I would like to suggest to you, that **Christmas isn't Christmas without Christ**.

I once read of a church notice board which had a cartoon on it. Two friends were pictured on the poster walking past the church.

"Look at that, Ethel," one woman said to her friend. "They're even bringing religion into Christmas."

And that just about sums up Christmas for the vast majority of people in 21st century Britain, doesn't it? A Christmas without religion. A Christmas without Christ.

So often nowadays we see or hear the word X-mas instead of Christmas, don't we?

But it is time to put Christ back into Christmas and to see what Christmas really means. It is time to understand what it is we are really celebrating. It is time to grasp the real reason for the season, the true meaning of Christmas.

It is time to also ask and answer that more fundamental question, "Are you **really** ready for Christmas?"

You see, the plays, the nativities, the school concerts we have mentioned can be lovely on a human level when we watch our children or grandchildren taking part. But they tell us nothing about the meaning of Christmas, only about some of the things that happened on that first Christmas Day and the days that followed.

So Christmas. Such a busy, frantic time. What then is it really all about?

Perhaps someone reading this book is wondering what your Christmas has really got to do with the birth of a baby born in a far-off land about two thousand years or so ago?

Let me take you back to 1982 just for a moment. It was the middle of winter. A young couple were excitedly awaiting the arrival of their first child. They lived in Berkshire and when the time had come for the baby to be born, they travelled to the hospital in Reading where their beautiful baby girl was delivered. The parents, Michael and Carole, named their child Catherine.

It was indeed a wonderful event for this young couple but at that time a seemingly insignificant event for the rest of the world. Fast forward if you will some 30 years. Only now can we make sense of this story. I'm sure you have worked out that the baby born in a Berkshire hospital grew up to marry a prince, and at the time of writing is now known as Catherine, Duchess of Cambridge. If the line of succession continues as we expect, she will one day be Queen and has already given birth to a future king.

We can thus readily see that a seemingly insignificant event, an ordinary event, can sometimes have serious consequences as time goes by.

You see, the real true story of Christmas has very little if anything to do with what Christmas has now become in the 21st century. It is very far removed from what we see around us today.

So, let us now consider two questions:

1. Who is this Jesus, born 2,000 years ago?
2. Why did Jesus appear on earth?

What Luke records in his thoroughly researched gospel is surely at the heart of the Christmas story and it tells us what it is really about.

> *And there were shepherds living out in the fields near by, keeping watch over their flocks at night. An angel of the Lord appeared to them, and the glory of the Lord shone around them, and they were terrified. But the angel said to them, 'Do not be afraid. I bring you good news of great joy that will be for all people.'"*[9]

The real story of Christmas is a story of good news, good news of great joy – and we all want to hear good news, don't we?

So, what is this good news?

This passage from Luke's Gospel tells us that a Saviour has been born.

This baby, born in Bethlehem, is no ordinary baby, you see. He was sent from Heaven by His Father. God had not sent a soldier or a judge or a reformer. No, He had sent a Saviour to meet man's greatest need.

Jesus was conceived of a virgin. Mary did not live with Joseph in a husband and wife relationship before Jesus was born. She was His earthly mother, the one in whose womb He was carried but Joseph was not his biological father. No, the Holy Spirit had come upon Mary and brought about this miraculous conception.

Straight away, then, we see that this child is set apart from all the rest of humanity. He is a unique being. He is God in human form. Matthew makes this clear:

[9] Luke 2:8-10

"Behold, the virgin shall conceive and bear a son,
and they shall call his name Immanuel"
(which means, God with us).[10]

God the Father waited for the right time in history to send His own Son in human form. Many passages in the Old Testament speak of the coming of a child in God's time. They point to the coming of a Saviour, a Messiah.

Now, Mary and Joseph had travelled around 80 miles to Joseph's hometown of Bethlehem which in those days would have been at least a 3 day journey! God's word was to be fulfilled. For 650 years before, the prophet Micah, in the Old Testament had prophesied or predicted the following,

"But you, Bethlehem Ephrathah,
though you are small among the clans of Judah,
out of you will come for me
one who will be ruler over Israel,
whose origins are from of old,
from ancient times."[11]

Now that time had come. The Son of God was born in real time, in a human body.

Good news was now brought to mankind that a Saviour had been born.

Let us go back to that scene some 2000 years ago. Try to imagine it. The night was dark, possibly cold. There were no streetlights, no electricity to give light in nearby farmsteads. The shepherds were in the fields guarding their sheep. Suddenly, an angel appears to them, a messenger from God. And more than that, the angel of the Lord appeared with the glory of the Lord, shining round about the shepherds. No wonder this was such a terrifying sight to them.

They were usually brave men, dealing with wild animals, used to dealing with the unexpected. But now they were terrified. The angel deals with this terror straightaway and tells them not to be afraid. Why was that? Why should they not be afraid? The angel goes on to give

---

[10] Matthew 1:23 English Standard Version
[11] Micah 5:2

the reason. They are not to be afraid because he, the angel, has not come to harm them but to bring them good news.

So, what is this good news and who is it for?

The good news will bring the shepherds great joy. Consider again Luke's account of the nativity. Luke records for us that this good news is not just for the shepherds, no, not at all! It is for all people – and that includes you and me!

> *But the angel said to them, "Do not be afraid. I bring you good news of great joy that will be for all the people.*[12]

Consider what Luke might have written next:

> *Today, in the town of David a baby has been born to you.*

That would have been a perfectly reasonable thing to announce. But just a moment. Look back at the verse again. That isn't what it says. Luke actually wrote:

> *Today in the town of David a Saviour has been born to you......*[13]

A Saviour has been born! A rescuer in other words. So, the shepherds, and all people who follow after them, are in need of rescuing. God had sent His angelic messenger to humble, despised shepherds with the most glorious message ever given. A Saviour has been born. And it is a glorious message for everyone today.

Now the shepherds would have understood what this meant. You see, they would regularly supply the lambs from their flocks to be used as sacrifices at the temple. There was a never ceasing need for animal sacrifices to seek forgiveness for sins committed.

But it was impossible, as it still is impossible, to satisfy a holy God's standard of perfection. The Bible tells us elsewhere that every person, that is each and every one of us, has sinned, has done wrong in God's sight.

We all know that, do we not? Let me illustrate this! If you are a mother or have had dealings with young children, you will know that a child doesn't have to be taught to be naughty or to want her own way, to sin as the Bible calls it.

---

[12] Luke 2:10
[13] Luke 2:11

Not one of us can ever be right with God by our own merits or good deeds. The shepherds were used to daily animal sacrifices to turn away God's anger and wrath but that was only a temporary solution. Another sacrifice would be needed tomorrow – and the next day; and the next; and the next.......

So, you may be wondering how a baby born in a Bethlehem stable can be the Saviour and the rescuer from our sin. Luke continues by telling clearly that this Saviour *"..... is Christ, the Lord."*

At last, the promised Saviour, the One waited for through many centuries of history, had come.

It is important to grasp that we are all in need of a Saviour, a rescuer. We all by nature are estranged from God. We all want to go our own way and live our life with no thought for the One who made us and before whom one day all will have to stand.

A Saviour has been born. His name is Jesus. He is Christ, the Lord. And everyone needs to come to Him in repentance and faith.

So, we have established who the baby is. And we have begun to look at why he came. To save, to rescue. How can a baby save the shepherds and the people from all nations down through the generations? Just as we fast forwarded 30 years in the life of Catherine Middleton, so we must do the same with the life of Jesus.

Thirty years or so after the birth of Jesus we come to what we now know as the Easter story. What has Christmas got to do with Easter, you might be thinking?

Christmas has everything to do with Easter. Jesus grew up to be a man. And just as He was unique amongst babies, so He is unique among men. We must refer to him as the God-Man because Jesus is both fully God and fully Man: 100% God; 100% Man!

You see, God had put an amazing plan of salvation in place before the world was created.

The amazing truth is that God became man when Jesus was born. The birth of Jesus was very special. His mother Mary was a virgin as we have seen. His birth was not the result of human love, or lust, but came about through the remarkable life-giving work of the Holy Spirit.

Salvation was planned in heaven, but it could not be accomplished in heaven. No man could atone for sin before a holy God, no man was qualified to do this since all men are sinners. So, the eternal God Himself became a man so that at His death on the cross He might accomplish salvation for His people. God became man so that as the man Jesus, He could die for His people and give to them the most amazing gift of all, salvation through His blood shed for them.

That plan meant that God's only Son, Jesus, who was perfect and without ever having sinned, had to die on the cross. This event took place on what we call Good Friday. And following that death Jesus rose again from the grave three days later – the day now called Easter Sunday. Death could not conquer Him – rather He had conquered death.

Jesus' birth was Act 1 of the plan, if you like. His death and resurrection made up Act 2. What an amazing and wonderful plan it was!

For Jesus was crucified and punished by His Father for your sins and mine. He stood in the place of sinful human beings. In doing so, He opened up the way for those who put their trust in Him to be restored to God, to have their sins forgiven, to have peace in their hearts, to call Almighty God Father and to spend eternity with Him in Heaven!

Why did He do this? It was all of love.

In what is probably the best known of everything written in the Bible we find this:

> *For God so loved the world that He gave His one and only Son, that whoever believes in Him shall not perish but have eternal life.*[14]

What was the response of the shepherds back in Bethlehem at the time of the birth of Christ?

Firstly, they believed what they had been told.[15]

Secondly, they acted upon what they had heard by going to see the baby for themselves.[16]

Thirdly, they glorified and praised God for all they had seen and heard ,which was just as they had been told by the angel.[17]

[14] John 3:16
[15] See Luke 2:15
[16] Luke 2:16
[17] Luke 2:20

I wonder, what will be your response to what you have read?

For those who are Christians, it should cause us to rejoice once again in our salvation, in the amazing grace which has been revealed to us in Christ our Saviour – to rejoice as the shepherds did!

And for any who do not know Jesus as their Saviour, what will be your response?

Will you, like the shepherds, believe the truth of this gospel, this good news? Will you act on this message by repenting of your sins and asking the Lord Jesus into your heart and life so that you too will know Him as your own Saviour and Lord?

Will you rejoice and glorify God and praise Him for what He has done for you in this amazing plan of salvation?

Or will you say in your heart there is no room for the Lord Jesus? Will you go back to all the busyness of the Christmas season ensuring that you are ready for Christmas in this world's terms, but still leaving out the centre of Christmas, the Christ who came to die for you?

Will you really be ready for Christmas? You are only really ready when you put Christ back into Christmas and trust Him as your Lord and Saviour.

The words of this carol were written for Christmas over 150 years ago. I think they put all of this together so well and call on each one of us to open our heart to Christ.

THOU didst leave Thy throne
and Thy kingly crown,
when Thou camest to earth for me;
but in Bethlehem's home
was there found no room
for Thy holy nativity:
O come to my heart, Lord Jesus!
there is room in my heart for Thee.

2 Heaven's arches rang
when the angels sang,
proclaiming Thy royal degree;
but of lowly birth
cam'st Thou, Lord, on earth,
and in great humility:

3 The foxes found rest,
and the birds their nest,
in the shade of the cedar tree;
but the earth was the bed
for Thy weary head,
in the deserts of Galilee:

4 Thou camest, O Lord,
with the living word,
that should set Thy people free;
but, with mocking scorn,
and with crown of thorn,
they bore Thee to Calvary:
O come to my heart, Lord Jesus!
Thy cross is my only plea.

5 When heaven's arches ring,
and her choirs shall sing,
at Thy coming to victory,
let Thy voice call me home,
saying, 'Yet there is room,
there is room at My side for thee!'
And my heart shall rejoice, Lord Jesus,
when Thou comest and callest for me.

Emily Elizabeth Steele Elliott, 1836-97[18]

---

[18] The author, Emily Elliott, has only one hymn in *Christian Hymns*. She was the niece of the more famous hymn-writer Charlotte Elliott. She was born at Brighton in 1836 and wrote most of her hymns for the use of the choir and school of St. Mark's Church where her father was the rector. She was his third daughter.

4

Christmas

The children were putting on the annual nativity play. They had decided that to show the radiance of the new-born Saviour a light bulb would be hidden in the manger. At the appropriate moment, all the stage lights were to be switched off except that one light bulb. However, when the moment came, the boy controlling the lights was so nervous, he became confused and turned off all the lights! There was a moment's silence. Then, one of the shepherds called out, "Hey, you've switched off Jesus."

"You've switched off Jesus." It's easy to do that, isn't it? To switch off Jesus. To be caught up in the cultural approach to Christmas. To forget all about the true meaning of Christmas. To switch Jesus off in your mind, your thoughts, your actions. That's what so many people throughout Great Britain and indeed around the world will be doing again at Christmas. Switching off Jesus. Blocking Him out. Removing Him from all that they do concerning Christmas. Making Christmas something it was never meant to be. I wonder if anyone like that is reading this book?

Let's begin by asking a question,

"What do people in society today think is the meaning of Christmas?"

In other words, what does Christmas mean to most people in 21st century Britain today?

For many, possibly for most, it is a time for pleasure, for eating and drinking to excess, for partying and enjoying themselves in celebration of Christmas.

It is a time for spending a lot of money, sometimes money people haven't really got, on things they don't really need or even want. Many people go into debt and spend the following year paying off their credit card bill to buy, buy, buy. Consumerism and materialism reach their peak at this time of year.

For some, it is a time to brighten the dullness of winter with its long dark evenings and cold, wet days. So, they go to town with the Christmas tree, the lights and the decorations both in, and outside their house. They decorate their houses and gardens to make them as bright and cheerful as they can. As we look around, we see that the shops and shopping centres are equally bedecked in lights and decorations for many weeks before Christmas Day itself.

And then of course we come to Father Christmas. Christmas wouldn't be Christmas without this larger than life figure. He has now become the centre of Christmas for many people, particularly children and young people. And whatever you do, you mustn't question his existence or tell children the truth about Father Christmas – just a man dressed up in a red costume. Parents have been known to become angry and make complaints against any church minister or schoolteacher who dares to tell the truth and suggest otherwise.

So, Christmas in the eyes of people in the world round about is a time for spending, for pleasure and enjoying themselves, for eating and drinking often to excess. And a time for placing Father Christmas in the centre of it all.

He, I would suggest, has become the great impostor. He has overshadowed and usurped Christ's position. The Christ in Christmas has become the X factor, so we now hear of Xmas. Christ, the One whom Christmas is all about has been removed from Christmas in the eyes of the world.

So, let us now consider the true meaning of Christmas and look at what the Bible tells us about what we might call the first Christmas and what it is really all about. What is the true meaning of Christmas?

There's a slogan that is sometimes seen on some Christmas cards and other Christmas items which says, "Jesus is the reason for the season."

I wonder, does that come as a surprise to anyone reading this? Christmas is about Christ. It's about Jesus. That being the case, who exactly is this person Jesus Christ?

Let me take you back in time to about 2000 years ago, to the country of Israel.

You may know something about the birth of a baby at that time from your school days or Sunday School. Perhaps you learnt about the Christmas story from a nativity play at school.

But perhaps you don't know why we are making so much fuss about a baby born all that time ago here and now some 2000 years later. After all, you may be thinking, aren't babies being born every day of every year? What is so different about this particular baby?

Well, to answer that question, we need to turn to what is recorded of the story for us in the New Testament, in Matthew's Gospel.

In the gospel record compiled by Matthew he writes:

This is how the birth of Jesus Christ came about: His mother Mary was pledged to be married to Joseph, but before they came together, she was found to be with child through the Holy Spirit.[19]

The Bible is clear. The words are plain. "This is how the birth of Jesus Christ came about" it says. Now the actual birth itself was as normal as yours and mine. He was born out of the womb of Mary, His mother as any baby is born. But, and this may be the most vital 'but' you have ever heard, it was His conception that was anything but normal. In fact, it was a miracle. For Jesus' conception was a virgin conception. This is what sets this baby apart from any other baby who has lived or will live. This is what makes this baby so completely different from the rest of mankind.

What do I mean by that? A virgin conceived. The passage makes it crystal clear. Mary was expecting this child before she and Joseph came together, as the passage very sensitively puts it. In other words, they had not had a physical relationship. Mary was betrothed or engaged to Joseph when she was told by an angel sent by God that she was to have a child. Joseph was not the biological father of her child. No man was.

No, Mary was the human vessel that carried the baby which she had conceived through the Holy Spirit. I think at this point we realise we are here standing on holy ground.

The Biblical record makes it very clear to us that there was no possibility that Joseph was the father of Christ in the biological sense.

---

[19] Matthew 1:18

Now you and I, and every other human being, did not exist before that moment of conception when we were conceived in our mother's womb from an egg and a sperm.

But, and here again is another vital 'but', the Lord Jesus Christ did not come into existence at the time of this virgin conception of which we have just read. No, not at all. He has been for all time. He is and will be for all time, for all eternity. Remember earlier, we asked who this baby was, born 2000 years go? The Bible tells us the answer. He is God. God the Son. He existed for all time in heaven. He came to earth in the form of a human baby, carried by Mary yet still God because it was the Holy Spirit who came upon her and brought about this supernatural conception. It was Mary who was granted this tremendous privilege and honour of carrying in her womb the Son of God. Since He existed before the creation of man, how could He ever possibly be born of a human father and mother?

Clearly, Joseph, on hearing that Mary was pregnant would assume, understandably so, that Mary had been unfaithful to him as he was her fiancé and that she had had a physical relationship with another man, resulting in the conception of the child she was carrying. Matthew tells us how Joseph responded – what he intended to do:

> *Because Joseph her husband was a righteous man and did not want to expose her to public disgrace, he had it in mind to divorce her quietly.*[20]

Betrothal among the Jews at that time was as binding as marriage. We learn from the book of Deuteronomy that Mary could have been stoned by the innocent party but more usually the guilty party was divorced by the innocent one which is exactly what Joseph was intending to do.

He loved Mary and he wanted to avoid a scandal. The passage says he didn't want to expose her to public disgrace. He felt compassion for her. And he might well have gone ahead with his intention, had not God stepped in. Now another supernatural event occurs, for an angel sent by God tells Joseph that Mary has not betrayed him, she had not behaved in any immoral way. No, the angel

[20] Matthew 1:19

32

informs Joseph that Mary's child has been conceived not by a man but by the Holy Spirit.

This assurance by the angel of the Lord that Mary's pregnancy was from the Holy Spirit gives Joseph the confidence he needs to go ahead with the marriage. The text tells us he was a righteous man. His love for God and for Mary meant that he was willing to bear reproach and mocking for the sake of Christ.

Picture the scene for a moment. Think of the gossiping in the neighbourhood, talking about him and Mary expecting a child outside of marriage, as the people would have seen it! It's worth noting that Joseph showed great faith in believing the message he received from God through the angel in his dream. Later in Matthew's narrative we see how obedient Joseph was, to what he had been told to do, for he kept his relationship with Mary pure until after her baby was born.

> *When Joseph woke up, he did what the angel of the Lord had commanded him and took Mary home as his wife. But he had no union with her until she gave birth to a son.*[21]

The angel also tells Joseph the name of the baby. He was to be called Jesus. Why was that? The reason for this choice of name is clear and is given to us in the text. The name Jesus means Jehovah or "is salvation". He will save His people from their sins. Wow!! An angelic declaration of who Christ is: The Saviour, the One who has come to bring salvation to a lost world.

Verse 21 reads,

> *She will give birth to a son, and you are to give him the name Jesus, because He will save his people from their sins.*

With this name, the angel reveals to Joseph the central purpose of Christ's coming. It is to save, to bring salvation, to save us from our sins. He is the promised Saviour, Messiah, who had been promised in the Old Testament prophets' writings many hundreds of years before.

The Old Testament prophet Micah declares in chapter 5 verse 2,

> *"But you, Bethlehem Ephrathah,*
>> *though you are small among the clans of Judah,*
> *out of you will come for me*
>> *one who will be ruler over Israel,*

---

[21] Matthew 1:14-25a

whose origins are from of old,
     from ancient times."

Notice once again that this verse from the prophet Micah clearly tells us who Jesus is. He has another name, Immanuel, which means "God with us".

Perhaps you may be thinking that I've spent rather a lot of time on this point of the virgin conception. Let me just say this. The whole truth of the Christian Gospel, the good news of salvation in Christ, depends on this being true! For if Christ had been the product of a union between Mary and Joseph, or Mary and any other man for that matter, He would not be who He claimed to be, that is, the Son of God. He would have been no different from any other human being. But no. You see, He was God who had come to earth and become a man. He was God in human flesh coming to earth for your sake, and mine.

Christ, conceived of the Holy Spirit, is the sinless one. He is the only one who has no sin in Him, because of who He is. I hope now you can see how vital it is to get hold of and believe the truth of Jesus born to a virgin young woman.

So, we have established who Jesus is and that Christmas is about Him and Him alone. Not Father Christmas, or Santa, or any of the other things we were thinking of earlier.

But now we must ask another question.

Why did He come?

You see, His ultimate purpose in coming was to be the Saviour, to save His people from their sins.

Let's fast forward 30 years to the time of the death of the Lord Jesus Christ. This is the time of Easter in the Christian church calendar.

Jesus is put to death on the cross. Remember He is the sinless one. So why did He die? We know from reading the Bible that sin must be punished. It must be punished by God who is holy and just. The Bible tells us that each one of us is a sinner however good we may think we are. In the eyes of God, we have all broken his law and are all sinful by nature. We are separated from God because of sin. One day we will all die and then what happens to our eternal soul? All of us were destined for hell, for a lost eternity and God's punishment upon us.

But God put in place a wonderful rescue plan, a plan of salvation. And that plan centres totally on Jesus, for it was Jesus who took away that punishment when He died on the cross. He was punished by His own Father for sins He had not committed. He took upon Himself the punishment for your sins and mine. He who did not deserve punishment took it for those who did. The Bible makes it clear. The iniquities , or sins, of us all were laid on Him. One of our hymns has this line,

> In my place condemned he stood.
> Hallelujah, what a Saviour! [22]

You may be thinking, why? Why would He do such a thing? The answer is both profound and simple - because He loved us!

Just as the miraculous conception is vital in understanding the Gospel, so now we have the second vital part of the jigsaw, if you like. Jesus died on the cross, but on the third day, what we now call Easter Sunday, He rose again. That's right. He rose from the grave! In doing so, He showed His power, His might and His deity. He conquered death itself and eventually went back to His Father in heaven, from where He had come. And now we have a Man in the heavenly places who is praying for us!

So, what does Christmas mean to you?

I wonder what your response is to what you have read about Christmas and its true meaning. For, you see, each one of us has to respond in some way, personally, to this Gospel message about the coming of the Lord Jesus Christ.

If you are a Christian, this message will be a reminder to you of that amazing grace shown to you in the Lord Jesus Christ and your heart will be warmed and full of joy once more.

But what if you are an unbeliever?

How will you respond? What will Christmas mean to you as you go about making all your plans and preparations? You see, you will either accept the Lord Jesus as your own personal Saviour or you will reject Him. You will never be able to say that you didn't know about the Saviour and what He has done for you. The Gospel demands a response from you.

---

[22] Man of sorrows! What a name – Philip P Bliss, 1875

The Lord Jesus Christ loves you. He died for you so that you may see and understand the true meaning of Christmas. So that you will no longer think of it as being about Father Christmas, or Santa, or whatever else you put in the place of the Christ of Christmas. You will understand that it is about the loving Son of God who left the glory and splendour of heaven to come down to a lowly stable as a baby and to go to that cross and to die for you that you might have life for all eternity.

I said earlier that the Lord Jesus has done all that is needed to bring about forgiveness of sin and salvation, appeasing the wrath of a holy God. There is, however, one thing that He cannot do for you. That is to believe. You must do that for yourself.

A greatly loved verse in John's gospel tells us plainly:

> For God so loved the world that He gave His one and only Son, that whoever believes in Him shall not perish but have eternal life.[23]

Many gifts are exchanged at Christmas time. The greatest gift of all is the gift of salvation from God himself. But you must accept that gift!

Let me close with this story by way of illustration.

"A couple of Decembers ago" writes a Christian pastor, "I was sitting next to our Christmas tree on Boxing Day when I noticed a small box still sitting under the tree. I picked it up and read the label and it had my name on it.

'Oh,' I said, to anyone who might have been listening, 'there's a present here for me that I haven't opened'. I looked at the shape of the packet and knew what it was. A much-needed item for one of my hobbies, I still needed to open the gift if I was going to get any pleasure at all from it and make any use out of it."

And so it is with the gift of faith. Perhaps you've left that gift under the tree as it were for many years. Perhaps you've never noticed it before. Perhaps you have seen it and known about it, but chosen to ignore it. Perhaps until this very moment, you've never realised what it was, or never realised it was for you, or that you had need of it.

---

[23] John 3:16

I hope you will open this very special gift which is for you from God Himself. It is the gift of forgiveness of sins and a new life in the Lord Jesus Christ. I hope you will put your trust in Him in faith and belief. I hope you will rejoice when Christmas comes around again in the one who is the Christ of Christmas!

5

April 1st

April 1st. Nowadays it is known as April Fools Day.

April Fools Day is a tradition which seems to have started in 1582, in France. Before that date the New Year was celebrated on April 1st. At around this time, with the introduction of the Gregorian calendar, New Year's Day was moved to January 1st, as we now know it.

Many people refused to accept the new calendar and continued to celebrate the New Year on April 1st even though everyone else had already celebrated it on January 1st. These people were labelled "fools" by the rest of the general population. They were subjected to ridicule, were made the butt of many jokes and were often sent on "fools' errands". This evolved over many years into a tradition of prank playing as we now know it and spread from France to Britain and other parts of the world.

Of course, this is all seen as light-hearted and amusing. However, did you know that the Bible does not consider a fool or foolishness as amusing in any way at all? On the contrary, the Bible has a lot to say on the matter of being a fool. In fact, the word "fool" occurs 95 times in Scripture, the word "fools" 53 times and the words "foolish" and "foolishness" occur as well.

The book of Proverbs has much to say on the subject of foolishness and there is much we can learn from the wisdom contained within it.

Let us begin with "the fool" defined.

The word "fool" in the language of the world today usually means "stupid".

The dictionary states that a fool is a person who acts unwisely, someone portrayed as a jester or a clown, or an empty-headed person. The word is used in Scripture with respect to moral rather than intellectual deficiencies. The fool, as described throughout the Bible, is not so much lacking in mental powers, but as one who misuses the ones he or she has.

In Scripture, the fool is the person who casts off the fear of God and thinks and acts as if he or she can safely disregard the eternal principles of God's righteousness. A fool thus chooses to disregard God and His wisdom.

The goal of the book of Proverbs is to impart wisdom. If we want to know about wisdom, we must know what folly is.

Do you want to be wise? Then you won't want to be a fool, Biblically speaking.

So how exactly is the fool described?

Firstly, the fool is described as someone who denies the evidence.

There are two psalms in the Bible that begin with identical words:

> *The fool says in his heart,*
> *"There is no God."*[24]

There are many people around us today, some in eminent positions, scientists, politicians as well as the ordinary person in the street ,who say this, despite there being so much evidence to the contrary.

Secondly, the fool is described as someone who trusts in himself.

The fool in his own eyes can do no wrong.

The book of Proverbs has much to say about a fool:

> *The way of a fool seems right to him,*
> *but a wise man listens to advice.*[25]

Foolishly, he trusts in his own heart.

Or, again from Proverbs:

> *He who trusts in himself is a fool,*
> *but he who walks in wisdom is kept safe.*[26]

So, how does this apply to us? What can we do to avoid being a fool?

> *Trust in the LORD with all your heart*
> *and lean not on your own understanding;*
> *in all your ways acknowledge him,*
> *and he will make your paths straight.*[27]

---

[24] Psalms 14 and 53
[25] Proverbs 12:15
[26] Proverbs 28:26
[27] Proverbs 3:5-6

Thirdly, the fool is described as one who is deaf to instruction.

Fools despise wisdom and instruction. A fool cares only to tell others what he knows, for a fool thinks he knows everything. The things that fools know are soon known by everyone and everyone soon knows how foolish he really is.

In other words, the fool speaks out of turn, he often puts his foot in it, he often speaks first before he thinks. He will speak and not listen to others who might well know more than he does.

Proverbs also tells us that it would be a waste of our time and energy if we tried to share wisdom with a fool.[28]

The fourth description of the fool is of someone who cannot be disciplined.

What lies ahead for the fool? Well, Proverbs tell us he is destined for much punishment. Yet even when the fool is punished, he is unlikely to learn from attempts to correct him. He hates being corrected and shown where he is going wrong and this in itself is the height of folly.

Our fifth description is of one who is impulsive.

A fool is one who vents all his feelings. His wrath is soon known. His impulsiveness makes his folly worse.

> *A fool gives full vent to his anger,*
> *but a wise man keeps himself under control.*[29]

The sixth description is a sombre one, describing one who commits evil.

Evil is like a sport or a game to a fool. Fools even make fun of sin. So, it is very difficult to get fools to depart from evil.

> *A fool finds pleasure in evil conduct,*
> *but a man of understanding delights in wisdom.*[30]
> *Fools mock at making amends for sin,*
> *but goodwill is found among the upright.*[31]

Finally, a fool is one who is virtually unchangeable.

---

[28] *Do not speak to a fool, for he will scorn the wisdom of your words.*
[29] Proverbs 29:11
[30] Proverbs 10:23
[31] Proverbs 14:9

Despite the most extreme efforts to change the ways of a fool it is almost impossible to rehabilitate him. He hates turning away from evil. Indeed, Proverbs has sobering words on this matter:

> *Though you grind a fool in a mortar,*
> *grinding him like grain with a pestle,*
> *you will not remove his folly from him.[32]*

And, again

> *As a dog returns to its vomit,*
> *so a fool repeats his folly.[33]*

In other words, he cannot change his foolish ways. He continues in his foolish behaviour and makes the same mistakes over and over again.

So, what have we concluded so far?

A fool declares there is no God; he trusts in him or herself; is deaf to instruction; cannot be disciplined; commits evil and is virtually unchangeable.

Where does that leave us? These observations and warnings are in Scripture to encourage us to choose a better path in life.

Finally, the book of Proverbs gives this contrast between the wise person and the fool.

> *The wise inherit honour, [or glory[34]]*
> *but fools he holds up to shame.[35]*

So, here are a number of questions for you to consider:

What will be your inheritance?

Will you be remembered with shame or honour?

Honour and glory can be yours if you are willing to listen to God.

Four times the Old Testament makes statements about the source of wisdom:

> *"The fear of the LORD is the beginning of wisdom,*
> *and knowledge of the Holy One is understanding.[36]*
> *The fear of the LORD is the beginning of wisdom;*
> *all who follow his precepts have good understanding.*

[32] Proverbs 27:22
[33] Proverbs 26:11
[34] Glory is used in the NKJV in place of honour.
[35] Proverbs 3:35
[36] Proverbs 9:10

To him belongs eternal praise.[37]
The fear of the LORD teaches a man wisdom,
and humility comes before honour.[38]
...... The fear of the Lord—that is wisdom,
and to shun evil is understanding.[39]

Do you want to be wise? Then you need to start with fearing the Lord and putting your trust in Him. Then you will be truly wise.

The time spent looking at foolishness and wisdom would not be complete without turning for a brief moment to the New Testament.

For it is Jesus who takes up this theme in Matthew's gospel chapter 7. Here ,He likens the man who hears His words of salvation and puts them into practice to the wise man who built his house on a rock. When the strong winds blew and the flood waters rose, this man's house did not fall down for it had been built on a solid foundation.

But the person who hears Jesus' words and does not put them into practice is likened to the foolish man who built his house on sand. When the storm came, this house fell to the ground with a great crash for it had no solid foundation.

So, we must ensure that we do have a solid foundation in our lives. Our lives must be built on the rock of the Lord Jesus Christ. Only then will we be able to stand when the storms of life hit us. Only then will we spend eternity with Him in glory. Only then will we be wise men and women.

[37] Psalm 111:10
[38] Proverbs 15:33
[39] Job 28:28

6

Three words beginning with C

In this chapter, I want us to consider three words beginning with the letter C.

For the first C, we need to return briefly to Christmas. Christmas itself, of course, begins with C which is helpful, but the word I want us to think about is the word **crib**.

We celebrated Jesus' birth when He came to earth as a baby. We all know His mother placed him in a manger but for the purposes of alliteration, I'm going to use the word crib.

The image of Jesus as a baby being placed in a crib seems to simply underline the fact that He was human. We know, of course, that Jesus is God, but He condescended to come to earth as a human being, fully human, fully man and we know that humans start their life as babies in a **crib.**

There's an awful lot of hype and commercialism associated with Christmas, as I'm sure you'll agree. It's not to the same extent in the run up to Easter, but it is still creeping in, albeit to a lesser extent and it's growing as time goes on.

Do you enjoy Easter? We don't usually ask that question, at least not to the same extent as we ask if you enjoy Christmas, do we?

Let's think about Easter for a moment. It's a nice time of year, isn't it? It's associated with the end of winter and the start of spring. We look forward to seeing the daffodils and the crocuses in our gardens and hedgerows, brightening things up after the long, dark days of winter.

It's a very busy time of year, too, for the DIY stores as people begin to plan their gardens or start to paint their houses. The days are drawing out, lighter evenings are upon us and we begin to feel better.

Perhaps you enjoy Easter because you like to eat a lot of chocolates or hot cross buns or Easter Simnel cake. You might have a treasure hunt hiding chocolate eggs in the garden or around the house for your children or grandchildren. All these things are enjoyable and good in themselves.

But I wonder if you have ever stopped to consider what Christians celebrate at Easter? What is it really about? Why do they celebrate Easter and what is it they are really remembering when they do celebrate it?

You see, for Christians, Easter is the most important time in the church calendar. It is at the heart of Christianity. It is what sets it apart from all other world religions.

Though not yet as commercialised as Christmas, for most people in Britain today Easter is simply treated as a holiday; as a time for gardening and other household tasks. Easter has become largely a secular holiday and the true, real meaning of Easter has been lost or forgotten.

Let's look for a moment at some of the things that society considers to be what Easter is all about.

We will then look at our second word beginning with C and what the Christian Easter is really about, the Biblical account of what we call Easter and what it means for each one of us.

Firstly then, what are some of the things many people associate with being what Easter is about?

It may be interesting to notice here that many of our so-called Easter traditions are, in fact, derived from pagan traditions. What are some of these traditions?

1. Hot Cross Buns
People in ancient times worshipped the goddess of spring and of the dawn. Her name was Eostre. (Pronounced Eastrer). She was also the Saxon fertility goddess. The Saxons thought that the sun died in the winter and was born again in the spring. They believed that this goddess brought the spring and with it the sun became stronger. Some believe that the name Easter we use today came from her name Eostre. As a pagan tradition, it is the beginning of new life and growth after the cold winter months.

It was at the feast of Eostre that an ox was sacrificed. The ox's horns became a symbol for the feast. They were carved into the ritual bread. The original hot cross buns!!

Actually, the word "bun" is derived from the Saxon word "boun" which means "sacred ox". Later, the symbol of a symmetrical cross was used to decorate the buns. The cross represented the moon, the heavenly body associated with the goddess Eostre and its four quarters.

2. Easter rabbits and eggs

The rabbit and the egg were symbols of the Norse goddess Ostara. Both symbols represented fertility. From these, we have inherited the present-day customs and symbols of the Easter bunny and the Easter egg.

Dyed eggs also formed part of the rituals of the ancient, pre-Christian Babylonian mystery religions. The egg as a symbol of fertility and of renewed life goes back to the ancient Egyptians and Persians who also had the custom of colouring and eating eggs during their spring festivals.

All of these things are interesting from a historical point of view. However, let me underline here and make things crystal clear. These things are what Easter is **not** about, as far as the Christian is concerned.

It isn't about cute little fluffy chicks, nor does it have anything to do with Easter bunnies. It may surprise you to hear that it isn't even about Easter eggs, nice though they may be! Easter nowadays is commercialised, though to a lesser extent than Christmas. There are Easter cards, Easter eggs and special Easter cakes. Many people tell their children the Easter bunny has delivered their eggs which are in a basket waiting for them when they wake up, in a similar way to telling them Santa will fill their stockings.

Easter celebrates life and rebirth which is why we see lots of symbols of new life and fertility Easter such as the eggs, chicks and rabbits spoken of already. An egg is seen as representing new life because life hatches from an egg.

For most people, particularly children, Easter means chocolate eggs. The shops are full of bright Easter displays decorated with chicks, rabbits and flowers, all with the objective of selling chocolate eggs in huge numbers. 90 million chocolate eggs were sold in the UK in one year. Eating chocolate Easter eggs is definitely the most popular Easter tradition today.

But Jesus came with a very real purpose, because as well as being fully human, He was, and still is, also fully God. His purpose in coming to earth from heaven was to be Saviour to fallen mankind.

You see, Christmas would be nothing at all for the Christian, without Easter! Why do I say that?

To answer that question, we must come to the second word beginning with C. That word is **Cross.** Easter is all about the **cross** on which Jesus died at **Calvary**.

We turn to John's gospel for information about the cross:

> *Carrying his own cross, he went out to the place of the Skull (which in Aramaic is called Golgotha).[40]*

Also:

> *Pilate had a notice prepared and fastened to the cross. It read: JESUS OF NAZARETH, THE KING OF THE JEWS.[41]*

A little later John records for us that,

> *Near the cross of Jesus stood his mother, ...[42]*

Why is the cross so important to Christians? To answer that, we need to ask two supplementary questions:

The first one is "What happened on that first Easter weekend?" and the second one, "Why did it happen?"

What events took place as recorded for us in the Bible and also in other non-Christian historical documents?

Jesus was put to death by crucifixion on what has come to be known as Good Friday. His body was taken down from the cross and buried in a cave tomb. This tomb was guarded by Roman soldiers and an enormous stone was put over the entrance so that no one would be able to steal the body.

On the Sunday morning, (what we now call Easter Sunday) Mary Magdalene and later some of Jesus' disciples visited the tomb. They

[40] John 19:17
[41] John 19:19
[42] John 19:25

48

found, to their astonishment, that the stone had been rolled away and the body of Jesus had gone!

The women at the tomb were spoken to by an angel sent from heaven by God. He told them that Jesus had risen from the dead.

Suddenly, Jesus Himself appeared to them, telling them not to be afraid, but to go and tell the disciples they had seen Him and that they were to go to Galilee where they would see Him for themselves. Jesus was seen by other people for 40 days after He rose from the dead, something we call the Resurrection. God had physically raised Him from the dead. This is the heart of the Christian Gospel.

Secondly, **why** did this happen? And what does it mean for us?

The Bible tells us that everyone has sinned. You may think you are a good person and, perhaps compared with some people you are. But compared to a Holy God? No!

Sin, you see, entered the world right back at the beginning of time as we know it. What happened is recorded for us in Genesis, the first book of the Bible. Look at young children. No one has to teach them to be naughty or to do wrong. No, sin is innate. It is there from the day each of us is born.

And sin has to be punished. Our sin has to be punished.

In Old Testament times, before the birth of Christ, sin was dealt with by using the blood of bulls, goats or a spotless lamb as a sacrifice. The sacrifice was brought by the priest to atone for his own sins and those of the people of God, the Israelites. This was known as a sin offering. This was the old way of atonement. The blood atoned for the people's sins. What do I mean by this? The offering brought about forgiveness for the sins of the people and made amends for their wrongdoings.

Since our sin has to be punished, either we are punished for that sin or someone else is punished in our place.

And that someone was Jesus. You see, Jesus was not a sinner. He was the perfect sinless one. Ah, but you say, earlier you said that everyone born had sinned. And that is true, with one exception. How is it that He is without sin? How is it that he has no sin in Him at all? It is because of who He is. He is God. He is the only one, throughout history past and time in the future, not born with innate sin and not committing any sin during His lifetime. And because He was sinless,

He was the only one who needed no punishment Himself. He was the only one who could die on the **cross** of Calvary, on what has become known as Good Friday, and take away our sin and our need of punishment. He was punished in our place.

God the Father, a just God, had to see justice done. So, this amazing rescue plan was put in place before the world was made. This way of salvation is open to all who trust in the Jesus Christ as their personal Saviour.

The Bible says,

"Believe in the Lord Jesus, and you will be saved ......"[43]

But the story of Easter doesn't end there. We now come to our third word beginning with C, the word **crown**. There are three aspects to this word "crown" in the New Testament.

First, in the Gospels of Matthew, Mark and John, we read of a **crown of thorns**.

They stripped him [that is Jesus] and put a scarlet robe on him, and then twisted together a crown of thorns and set it on his head. They put a staff in his right hand and knelt in front of him and mocked him. "Hail, king of the Jews!" they said.[44]

It doesn't stop there though, as in Hebrews, the writer speaks of a **crown of glory and honour** which has been placed on Jesus' head.

We read,

You [that is God the Father] made him [that is God the Son, Jesus]
a little lower than the angels;
you crowned him with glory and honour

And again, we read,

But we see Jesus, who was made a little lower than the angels, now crowned with glory and honour because he suffered death, so that by the grace of God he might taste death for everyone.[45]

---

[43] Acts 16:31
[44] Matthew 27:28-29
[45] Hebrews 2:9

A crown of thorns placed by those who would mock and laugh at Him is now replaced by a crown of glory and honour placed by God the Father, as a reward for what He has done on Calvary for us.

So, Jesus who starts His life in a **crib,** who dies for us on a **cross**, finishes with what is rightfully His, with a victor's **crown** of glory and honour on His head.

We could stop there, marvelling at the wonder of it all and the amazing plan put into place by God before time began.

But there is a third way in Scripture where the word **crown** is used. It is the **crown** of life, at other times described as the **crown** of righteousness.

What does the Bible say? Let's look at some examples.

Paul, writing to Timothy says,

*I have fought the good fight, I have finished the race, I have kept the faith. Now there is in store for me the **crown of righteousness**, which the Lord, the righteous Judge, will award to me on that day—and not only to me, but also to all who have longed for his appearing.*[46]

In Peter's first letter we read,

*And when the Chief Shepherd appears, you will receive the **crown** of glory that will never fade away.*[47]

Then, in James' letter to the twelve tribes scattered among the nations, he says,

*Blessed is the man who perseveres under trial, because when he has stood the test, he will receive the **crown** of life that God has promised to those who love him.*

There are a number of similar words in Revelation. For example, writing to the church in Smyrna, John says,

*Do not be afraid of what you are about to suffer. I tell you, the devil will put some of you in prison to test you, and you will suffer persecution for ten days. Be faithful, even to the point of death, and I will give you the **crown** of life.*[48]

The recipient of the **crown** of life, righteousness or glory in the verses here is now not the Lord Jesus Christ. Who then is this crown

---

[46] 2 Timothy 4:7-8
[47] 1 Peter 5:4
[48] Revelation 2:10

for? Well, the promises in these verses are for the followers of Jesus. For those who know Him as their Saviour and Lord. For those who love Him and are obedient to His teachings and His word.

It is for all those who have put their trust in Jesus and don't give up when sufferings and trials come.

A number of passages in the Bible refer to the Christian life as a race. For example, in the first letter to the Corinthians, Paul writes,

*Do you not know that in a race all the runners run, but only one gets the prize? Run in such a way as to get the prize. Everyone who competes in the games goes into strict training. They do it to get a crown that will not last; but we do it to get a **crown that will last for ever**.*[49]

How true that is. So many people in the world are striving for prizes that will not last. Sport, stardom in music or theatre, whatever it might be. Chasing after that which is temporary. I wonder, what is it that you are striving for?

We must seek to run the race of faith, where one day we will be rewarded with that crown of life which will be ours for ever and for eternity.

So, what does it mean for you reading this today? All there is for you to do is to come to Jesus in faith. To acknowledge that you are a sinner in the sight of God and to ask for His forgiveness. There is nothing you can do to earn salvation, or to take away your own sin. No, all that is needed has already been done for you by Christ.

What will Easter be about for you next time it comes around in the calendar?

You must decide. Will it be all about chocolate and the Easter traditions we considered at the beginning? Or will it be about Christ, the One who went from crib, to cross to crown.

Will it be about the Saviour who gave His life for you that you might have eternal life with Him and one day have the crown of righteousness, the crown of life placed on your head?

[49] 1 Corinthians 9:24-25

54

7

When "What" becomes "Even"!

What if? What if?

I'm sure we have all heard those words at some time or another, perhaps many times? Maybe you have said them yourself, perhaps many times.

Have you ever found yourself feeling fearful? I'm sure you have, as I have.

Not necessarily a heart stopping, all-encompassing type of fear, but the kind of gnawing anxiety that occurs when you think about the future and all that it might hold.

You begin to wonder, "**What if?**"

"What if the worst happens? What if this should happen? What if that should happen?"

Am I right? We all do it, don't we?

I'm sure we have all thought it, said it, at least once and perhaps many times during the course of our life and perhaps increasingly so as we get older.

The question, "What if?" has a way of unsettling us, of unnerving us, of destroying our peace and leaving us feeling insecure and troubled. Wouldn't you agree?

Is this a new situation? Is it something particularly associated with today's way of life with its stresses and pressure? Not at all!

People in the Bible were uneasy about things in their situation too and they asked **what if**? questions.

Let's look at some examples for a moment. The phrase "**what if**" appears 17 times in the Scriptures.[50] The first time it is used is right back in the book of Genesis. Six times Abraham uses these words when he pleads with God to spare the righteous in Sodom.

---

[50] As in the NIV, 1984 Anglicised edition

For example, Abraham asks **what if** there were a number of righteous people there – what would God do then? He pleads with God, saying,

What if only ten can be found there?[51]

And the gracious Lord answers,

For the sake of ten, I will not destroy it.[52]

Abraham was so concerned that if there were godly people among the wicked in Sodom, they would all be destroyed so he asks God to intervene and not destroy the city.

A few chapters further on in Genesis we read of the now aged Abraham wanting to be assured of a wife for his son Isaac from among his own people and so he plans to send his servant back to his relatives to procure such a wife from among them.

But what do we read of the servant and his understandable concerns? The servant said to Abraham,

What if *the woman is unwilling to come back with me?*[53]

Again, in Genesis, in the well-known story of Joseph, Joseph's brothers ask,

What if *Joseph holds a grudge against us?*[54]

All of them were wondering what would happen if circumstances went awry, just as we do.

Even the great Moses, chosen by God to lead His people out of captivity from Egypt, was not immune from the anxieties of "what if?"

Moses, when told by God to lead the Israelites out of Egypt, asked the question,

What if *they do not believe me or listen to me and say, 'The Lord did not appear to you'?*[55]

We all face a huge array of "**what ifs**", don't we? Some might be minor issues while others would have life changing repercussions.

---

[51] Genesis 18:32
[52] *Loc. cit.*
[53] Genesis 24:39
[54] Genesis 50:15
[55] Exodus 4:1

What if my child dies? **What if** my health goes, or I get cancer? **What if** my spouse were to leave me? And so on. You can put your own concerns after those two words, I'm sure.

The truth, whether we like it or not, is that any of these things could happen. There are no guarantees for any of us. The Bible does not promise us an easy life. Far from it.

But if any or all of these things that we dread do happen to us, we must ask ourselves this searching question, "Is God enough?"

If our deepest fears are realised, will God still be sufficient? Or will our god (notice the small g) collapse alongside us as we cave in under the weight of the burdens and sorrows that come our way?

These are serious questions that we all need to face up to.

If our health deteriorates, if we end up in care, will God be enough?

What if my children or grandchildren rebel and do not walk with the Lord? Will God be enough then?

If my suffering, whatever that might be, continues and I never see the purpose in it, will God still be enough?

Think for a moment of the worst thing you fear most. If that happened to you, would God be enough for you in the midst of that situation?

Of course, we want to say 'yes', God **is** sufficient for all these things. If we are truly honest with ourselves however, do we not struggle? We don't want to give up our dreams, we don't want to surrender those things that are dear to us, we don't want to relinquish what we might feel we are entitled to.

Is it not true that often part of our desire to be faithful to God is so that we get payback? We expect something back from God. Do we perhaps fall into the way of thinking that surely God owes me something? That is to think in an unbiblical way.

For you see, we are called on as Christians to love God for who He is, not for what He can do for us. We are called on to worship Him for who He is because He is worthy and because He is God.

When we relinquish our expectations to His sovereign will, He reminds us that we have something far better than a reassurance that our dreaded "**what ifs**" won't happen.

This is where "**What**" becomes "**Even**". Or to be more precise, when "**what if**" becomes "**even if**".

The Lord gives us the assurance that **even if** these things do happen to us, He will be there in the midst of them. He will carry us. He will comfort us. It is He who will strengthen us and will tenderly care for us. He will provide for us.

God doesn't promise us an easy life, one which is trouble free. But He does promise that He will be there in the midst of our suffering and sorrows.

So, this is where our **what** becomes **even**, our **what ifs** become **even ifs**.

Let us go on to consider what the Bible says about **even if**.

Turn again to the Scriptures where we can consider some examples of how this **even if** works out in practice.

"**Even if**" appears almost 60 times in the Scriptures. I've picked out a few of the more relevant ones. I want us to see as we move through the verses the link between the "what if" and the "even if".

Remember the story of Shadrach, Meshach and Abednego recorded in the book of Daniel. There was no guarantee that they would be delivered from the fiery furnace but just before Nebuchadnezzar delivered them into the flames of the fire, they spoke some of the most courageous words ever uttered:

> *If we are thrown into the burning furnace, the God whom we serve is able to deliver us from it. But, **even if** He does not, we want you to know that we will not serve your gods.*[56]

How amazing is that! They could have said,

"Oh, **what if** we don't get out alive? **What if** we can't cope with the terrible pain, the heat and anguish?"

But no! They did not ask **what if** the worst happened to them. They did not ask **what if** at all.

Those three young men faced the fiery furnace without fear because they knew that whatever the outcome, (and they had no way of knowing for certain what that would be), they were in God's hands and it would ultimately be for their good and for God's glory. They were satisfied knowing that **even if** the worst happened to them, God

[56] Daniel 3:17-18

58

would be with them and would take care of them. What faith! The Bible tells us that **even if** the worst happens to us, whatever that might be, God's grace is sufficient for us.

Paul suffered from some physical ailment which he calls a "thorn in the flesh". It was a hindrance to him. Having pleaded three times with the Lord to take away what he calls the thorn in his flesh (we don't know what that was), he writes,

But he [that is God] said to me, 'My grace is sufficient for you, for my power is made perfect in weakness'.[57]

Paul goes on to say that he, Paul, will boast all the more gladly about his weaknesses, so that Christ's power may rest on him. That is why, he says, for Christ's sake, he delights in weaknesses, in insults, in hardships, in persecutions and in difficulties, for when he is weak then he is strong. Not strong in himself, of course, but in the power of Christ. That power and grace is still sufficient for us today if we put our trust in Christ and cast all our cares on Him.

Even if.

Those two words, those two simple words have taken the fear out of life. Replacing "**what if**" with "**even if**" is one of the most amazing things we can do. It is one of the most important exchanges we can ever make. If we do this, we will be changing our fears of an uncertain, changeable future for the loving assurance of an unchanging God.

We will see that **even if** the worst happens, God will carry us through. He will still be God. He has promised He will never leave us.

Let us look at another Biblical example. Think of Habakkuk for a moment. He demonstrates this exchange of **what if** for **even if** beautifully.

For those of you unfamiliar with this Old Testament prophecy, here are just a few brief words by way of explanation. In the first chapter, Habakkuk complains to the Lord. How long, he says, must I call for help and plead with you, O God, to save my people? How long, he asks the Lord, will you tolerate wrong and injustice and allow the wicked to pervert the cause of justice? The Lord answers him in

---

[57] 2 Corinthians 12:9

a mighty way. but Habakkuk complains again, in chapter two. Then the Lord shows him who it is that is in control.

> The Lord is in His holy temple; let all the earth be silent before Him.[58]

So, in the third and final chapter, we have recorded for us Habakkuk's prayer where he closes his prayer and his book with these words,

> For **even if** the fig tree doesn't blossom,
> and no fruit is on the vines,
> **even if** the olive tree fails to produce,
> and the fields yield no food at all,
> **even if** the sheep vanish from the sheep pen,
> and there are no cows in the stalls;
> still, (**YET**) I will rejoice in (the Lord),
> I will take joy in the God of my salvation.
> (the Sovereign LORD) is my strength! [59]

We can't leave the **even ifs** of the Old Testament without considering for a moment the life of Job. Remember the story of Job and all that he had to suffer: his great loss in terms of family, children, sheep and cattle and other belongings and in terms of health. So much trouble heaped on one man. So much to break him and cause him to harden his heart against God. So much to cause worry, anxiety and to cause him to say, 'What if?'

And yet, is that what we read of Job? No, not at all. What does he have to say in all of this?

> Though (**Even if** is the sense) He (that is, God) slay me, yet will I hope in him; ....[60]

Even if God were to kill him, says Job, he will still hope and trust in Him. After all that he had been through, and with no knowledge of how his future was going to turn out, this was Job's testimony. I wonder, is it yours?

There are a number of New Testament verses which brings all this clearly into focus.

---

[58] Habakkuk 2:20
[59] Habakkuk 3:17-19a, as translated in the *Complete Jewish Bible*
[60] Job 13:15

Peter, who describes himself as one of Jesus' apostles, wrote two letters to first century Christians In the first of those letters, he writes,

Who is going to harm you if you are eager to do good? But **even if** *you should suffer for what is right, you are blessed. "Do not fear what they fear; do not be frightened." But in your hearts set apart Christ as Lord. .....[61]*

Here then is the crux of the matter, is it not? It's not really about us at all. It's all about Christ. Whatever we have to face today, tomorrow or in the years to come that God grants us we will be blessed in our suffering if we put the Lord Jesus Christ at the centre of our life.

So how does all this work out in practice for us today? How does it help us live a Christian life in the way the Bible would have us do? Let's look at the practical outworking for us. What are the practical outcomes if we replace "**what if**" with "**even if**"?

Can I suggest three ways in which our lives will be changed?

Firstly, we will know peace in our hearts. We noted earlier that the **what if syndrome** robs us of peace and fills us with worry and anxiety. Instead, the way opens up for us to have that amazing peace restored. It will bring a calm spirit within us and enable us to cope with all that we have to deal with.

Secondly, we can claim the promise of God's presence with us. If we are constantly fretting and concerning ourselves about what might or might not happen, we will not live in a way that exhibits God's presence with us in our daily walk. But when we embrace the **even if** outlook and way of thinking, God will again fill us with His peace and love and will be with us wherever we go, as His word promises.

Then thirdly, our heavenly Father knows all our needs and He gives us very many promises in Scripture to encourage us and help us on our earthly pilgrimage.

Someone reading this may feel this sounds exactly what they need, but may be wondering how to go about making these changes.

For the Christian believer, there are only two things to do. It is essential to study God's word, the Bible and spend time in prayer. Nothing terribly new, but perhaps a timely reminder.

---

[61] 1 Peter 3:13-15a

When we read God's word, when we immerse ourselves in it and meditate upon it daily, we are fed spiritually. We are given all that we need to enable us to trust God and to be encouraged and strengthened by it.

When we pray, we come closer to God and learn to leave our earthly concerns at the cross. Or another way of putting it, is to say we can leave them at the throne of grace where Scripture tells us we can find mercy and grace to help in time of need. If we spend time with the Lord in prayer, we can hand our fears, our anxieties and worries over to Him. We can remind ourselves on a daily basis of who He is and what He has already done for us in the Lord Jesus Christ, in saving us and forgiving us all our sins. We can remind ourselves that He is the same God, yesterday, today and forever.

So, a life full of **What if?** is one where we are not trusting in God, whereas a life full of **Even if** is a life trusting in the Lord.

It all comes down to a matter of trust; of faith and belief and taking God at His word.

Do you believe in such a God? Do you have faith in such a God? Have you put your trust in the Lord Jesus Christ?

Trust Him; take Him at His word and you will be saved. Then all your **what ifs** will be changed to **even if**. And instead of saying **what if** this or that happens, we will be able to say **even if** this or that happens, we will have peace in our hearts from God and will be able to be strengthened and supported by His promises which never fail.

Then, we will be able to say with Job, "**Even if** He slay me, yet I will still hope (trust) in Him."

8

"The LORD is my Shepherd"

Psalm 23

I wonder what comes to your mind when you think of sheep. Clearly not noted for their brilliance, sheep are gifted wanderers. They get caught in thickets, end up lost, are vulnerable to attack from wolves and tend not to march in orderly lines. You get the picture? Not particularly complementary, is it? Clearly in need of ---- a shepherd.

I want you to think of yourself, at least for the moment, as a sheep. It will help as we seek to learn from the Scriptures about the One who is our Shepherd.

The dictionary gives the following as definitions of a shepherd:
- ➤ a person who herds, tends and guards sheep.
- ➤ a person who protects, who guides or watches over a person or group of people.
- ➤ a member of the clergy.
- ➤ The Shepherd, Jesus Christ.

Perhaps the last one was unexpected in a secular dictionary!

But Jesus Christ is exactly the person that we need to focus on as we look more carefully at Psalm 23.

The 23rd Psalm is probably the most well-known and well-loved of all the psalms.

David, its author, wrote this psalm to express his confidence in the Lord's care for him.

¹ The LORD is my shepherd, I shall not be in want.
² He makes me lie down in green pastures,
he leads me beside quiet waters,
³ he restores my soul.
He guides me in paths of righteousness
for his name's sake.

⁴ Even though I walk
  through the valley of the shadow of death,
I will fear no evil,
  for you are with me;
your rod and your staff,
  they comfort me.
⁵ You prepare a table before me
  in the presence of my enemies.
You anoint my head with oil;
  my cup overflows.
⁶ Surely goodness and love will follow me
  all the days of my life,
and I will dwell in the house of the LORD
  for ever.

As he reflected on that care, David saw that it was very much like the care of a shepherd for his sheep in verses 1-4, and also like the care of a host for his house guests, as in verses 5-6.

Both of these things were of course very familiar to David. You remember that as a boy he cared for his father's sheep and later on as King David, he would host many guests in his palace.

In the psalm, the "boot is very much on the other foot" (or perhaps in David's case we should say the sandal is on the other foot!) For now, David is not the shepherd he once was, but is one of God's sheep. Or to be more accurate, he is one of the Lord Jesus Christ's sheep, for it is He who is described in the New Testament as the Good Shepherd. David is no longer the one who is the host but is now the guest in the presence of none other than the Lord God Himself. He is the host!

Many have described this psalm as a psalm of privilege! What an amazing privilege it is, to read of the Lord God Himself, caring for His people as a shepherd and a host. Throughout the psalm, we see what God does for His people.

It's important to note that this psalm is not a prayer. David is not asking God to do something for him. No, he is rejoicing, celebrating if you like, what the Lord Jesus has done and will continue to do in his life.

Let's have a look at the psalm more closely.

The first four verses describe David's confidence in the care of the LORD as a shepherd.

David begins with these wonderful words:

The Lord is my shepherd. I shall not want.

Pause and think about this for a moment. It is so easy to miss the blessing of passages which are very familiar to us, such as these words are.

Consider for a moment what is being said here. The Sovereign Lord of the universe has become a shepherd to David! We can only assert such a thing because the Lord has chosen to reveal Himself in such a way in other parts of Scripture.

In John's Gospel, for example, we read of Jesus saying,

I am the Good Shepherd. The Good Shepherd lays down His life for the sheep.[62]

What care and love is this?

Through His redeeming death on the cross, Christ purchased His sheep. He paid the ultimate price by laying down His own life on the Cross of Calvary. The wrath of God for sin -David's sin, your sin and my sin - was taken for us by Christ. It was as if Christ the Shepherd stepped in between His sheep and His father, and took the wrath of God on Himself, on behalf of His sheep.

What does this mean for each of us?

The sheep have been bought by Jesus through His death on the cross and now He lovingly tends them. For those of us who are Christians, when we read verse 1, we see the Lord Jesus as our Shepherd.

David describes the care he has received from the Lord as the best possible care from the best possible Shepherd, the Lord Jesus Himself, of course.

I wonder if you can say with David,

"The Lord is my Shepherd"?

You see, that it is a very personal response. The verse speaks of a personal shepherd.

David celebrates the Lord's care for him both in life in verses 1-3, and in death in verse 4.

---

[62] John 10:11

In what way did the Lord care for David in life?

The Lord provided David with everything he needed in life. Notice, everything he **needed**, not **wanted**. And it is the same for believers today.

Four distinct needs are mentioned here.

1: Food

The psalm is speaking in verse 2, of course, about spiritual food. The green grass spoken of here is speaking of food for our souls.

The green pastures, the green grass the sheep need is the word of God.

As we spend time meditating on the Scriptures, as we listen when the word of God is soundly preached, we are being fed, spiritually speaking. The Lord is providing green pasture for those who are His sheep every time the word of God is truly preached.

I wonder, do we avail ourselves of every opportunity to be fed in this way? Do we attend the services that are available to us whenever we possibly can to hear Biblical preaching? Or do we stay away, and, in doing so, stray from the Good Shepherd and fail to benefit from the food He has provided for us?

2: Refreshment

Verse 2 continues,

He [the LORD] leads me beside quiet waters.

In other words, the sheep do not lack spiritual refreshment. They and we are in need of such refreshment because we walk in a wearying, exhausting world. Even our fellow sheep, that is our fellow believers can weary us at times, and cause us to be in need of refreshment.

Where is this refreshment to be found?

Once again, we find all that we need to refresh us in the word of God. Back to the Bible again we must go to find green pasture on which to feed and refreshing water from which to drink.

In what ways do the Scriptures refresh us? How about these to get us started?

➢ When we think about the greatness of God
➢ When we meditate and marvel at His glorious plan of salvation

- ➢ When we consider that He loved us from the beginning of time
- ➢ When we remember that He sent His only Son the Lord Jesus Christ to be our Saviour and Redeemer, to die in our place at Calvary
- ➢ When we consider that Jesus continues to pray for us to His Heavenly Father
- ➢ When we remember the glorious promises made in the Scriptures, not least of which is that He will return again and take us to be with Him in eternity, for ever and ever.

Are not all these things wonderful means of refreshment for our souls? Do you know something of having your spiritual thirst quenched in this way? Or is this all a mystery to you?

3: Forgiveness and Renewal

In the third verse we discover that the sheep do not lack forgiveness and renewal because their souls are restored.

We know that sheep can stray from the fold, and followers of the Lord Jesus Christ can be known to stray also. But the Lord still cares for His own whether they stay close to Him or whether they have strayed.

David himself strayed far from the Lord but was never beyond the saving grace of his Shepherd, the Good Shepherd.

You may remember the events in the New Testament which led to the fall of Simon Peter. He had been so close to Jesus yet still strayed from Him. We also know though that Simon Peter was pursued, forgiven and restored by his Good Shepherd.

Any one of us who names the name of Christ as our own personal Saviour can still fall; we can still stray from Him, but His amazing grace will draw us back to His side for He knows His sheep by name.

4: Direction and Guidance

Lastly, the sheep do not lack direction and guidance because they are led by the Lord Jesus Christ in paths of righteousness. We see this in verse 3:

> *He guides me in paths of righteousness*
> *for his name's sake.*

How wonderful is this part of the shepherd's care! He has promised to lead His people.

It is important to pause here and note that the Lord always leads His people in **paths of righteousness**, that is, in ways which always concur, always agree with His will in the Scriptures. Once again, we are brought back to the Bible!

If you are seeking guidance in your life or seeking to know God's will in any given situation, always remember we can never claim to be guided by God for actions or decisions that contradict His word. If we are walking close to God, we will know His will as He will lead us. He has promised to do so.

Consider again the words of verse 3 quoted above.

What does this mean? It means He guides His people according to all that His name represents. He guides us in keeping with His holiness, His love, His faithfulness, His wisdom and everything else we know about His character as revealed to us in the Scriptures.

Now let us look at the Lord's care for David and therefore for the Christian believer, in death. Look again at verse 4:

> *Even though I walk*
> *through the valley of the shadow of death,*
> *I will fear no evil,*
> *for you are with me;*
> *your rod and your staff,*
> *they comfort me.*

It is natural for us to fear physical death. But David tells us that once again the Lord, His Shepherd is with him even in a situation like death which would naturally fill him with terror.

The verse speaks of the shadow. A dark shadow can appear to be quite a frightening thing but in its own right it cannot hurt us; it has no power to harm us in any way.

And death, frightening and forbidding as it surely is, cannot ultimately do us any harm or hurt us, if we are one of God's children. If we are one of His sheep whom He has cared for in life, then He will continue to care for us as we die.

Death is like the shadow; it cannot harm us because Christ has removed its sting, leaving only the shadow.

David describes death as walking. There is no panic here, no frenzy, no rushing about in a state of terror. No, a restful, gentle walk. And where is the walk? In the valley of the shadow of death.

Notice again that word "through". How encouraging is that word. The valley of death is something the Christian believer is passing through, travelling along to get to a better place on the other side of the valley. It is not a final resting place. It is not somewhere for the child of God to stop. No, we are walking through and will be brought to safety by God, to be with God.

How was David able to say such things?

It was because David's peace concerning death came from one source and one source only, the Lord Himself.

Consider verse 4 again. As David contemplates death, he realises that the Lord is with him. He has nothing to fear.

Not only that, David sees that the Lord is carrying a rod and a staff. What is the significance of these two items?

The rod was a heavy club used by shepherds to kill any wild animals that might be tempted to attack the sheep. The staff was a long pole with a crook at one end which the shepherds used to round up the sheep and guide them along to the right place. Do you get the picture? Can you see it in your mind's eye?

Both of these items represent safety, protection and guidance. Thus, David could say without a shadow of a doubt that he would not be afraid.

Not afraid of what, exactly?

He would not be afraid of his enemies of doubt, of guilt, of any kind of evil as he knew that his Shepherd, the Lord Jesus Christ was there with His rod in His hand to kill them off. Similarly, he would not be afraid of death itself because he knew the Lord would guide him in death as He had in life with His staff in His hand.

For each one of us to have the same peace in our hearts about death, we must be able to say as David did in verse 1,

The LORD is MY Shepherd.

In other words, we must know the Lord Jesus Christ as our own personal Saviour and Lord and put our trust in Him, as we live out this life and look ultimately to the next.

If we want the peace that David had, we must have the faith that David had.

We must recognise our need of the Good Shepherd, the Lord Jesus Christ.

We must rely totally upon Him and on no other earthly shepherd, on no prime minister or other politician or on anyone or anything else this world has to offer us.

This brings us to the last two verses of the psalm.

David now reveals his confidence in the Lord's care as a host.

The illustration David uses now changes. We are no longer seen as sheep in God's flock. Now, for those of us who are God's children we are described as guests at a banquet. You see, if we are Christians, we are now God's friends. How wonderful! How amazing is that?

Once we were enemies, born in trespasses and sins, the Bible tells us. Now, through what Jesus did for us on the cross of Calvary, we are brought back to God and into His family.

The host of a banquet provides for his guests. In verse 5, we see God as the banqueting host, firstly in this life and later on in the life to come:

You prepare a table before me
in the presence of my enemies.
You anoint my head with oil;
my cup overflows.

God provides for His people in this life. As we make our way through this earthly pilgrimage, we face enemies. Enemies, that is, of our soul. There are those who would seek to destroy us, if not physically then spiritually. The world seeks to pull us down. The devil is roaring like a lion, seeking to devour those who have faith in Christ. Our own sinful flesh is something we battle with on a daily basis.

David is declaring here that God cares for His people in all these circumstances and situations. God is the ultimate Host!

How does David express it?

You anoint my head with oil; my cup overflows.

It was the ancient custom in the time of David to anoint the heads of kings at their coronation and at the installation into office of the High Priest.

But it was also used to welcome a guest by anointing that person with olive oil mixed with fragrant perfume and costly spices. The host was showing his guest that nothing was too much trouble, that no expense would be spared, that he was being made extremely welcome.

Here the psalmist is speaking of himself as an honoured guest of the Lord Himself. It is the Lord who prepares a table for him, is hospitable to him by anointing him with oil, and in such abundance that his cup is overflowing.

David is so taken up with this astonishing, amazing truth of the care of his Heavenly Father that he writes in the final verse:

Surely goodness and love will follow me
all the days of my life.

He knew he could count on God's care and love every step of the way.

Finally, David concludes by saying,

I will dwell in the house of the Lord for ever.

This really is the climax of the whole psalm. This is what it has all been about.

God's care for His people in this life is but a foretaste of what is in store for them when they reach their final destination, and receive their glorious reward, in Heaven itself.

One day all believers will sit at the Lord's table in the everlasting kingdom. There will be no enemies there to deal with. There will be no doubts, no sin, and no guilt. Those who are fully trusting in the Saviour will then fully understand the extent of His goodness and love, and what it really meant for Him to die in our place. We will see Him face to face.

David knew all this would one day be his.

We can know this too, if we accept Christ as our own personal Saviour, our Good Shepherd, our Lord and Master.

May the Lord enable each reader to do so.

And for those who already trust Him in this way, once again our hearts can be filled with the joy and wonder of it all, and we can give Him all the praise and glory that is due to His name.

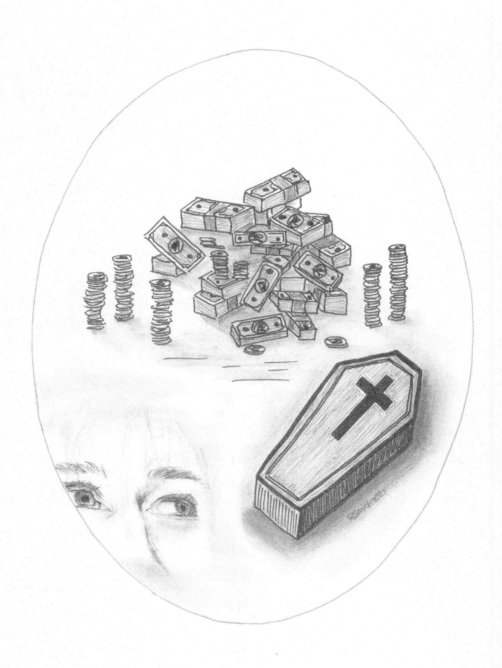

9

"Then I understood"

Psalm 73

I wonder if, like me, you have looked around you at other people for whom life always seems easy and everything always seems to run smoothly. We may think how unfair this is, especially when life is perhaps hard, and the going is tough for us.

If you have, you will be in good company, for that is exactly how the psalmist was thinking when he wrote Psalm 73. He tells us that he has gone through an experience which has left him badly shaken, so much so that he nearly fell.

> But as for me, my feet had almost slipped;
> I had nearly lost my foothold.[63]

Why was this?

Well, he had become aware of something that had caused him great pain. Here he was living a godly life. He had avoided sin and spent time in prayer, confessing his sin and seeking forgiveness. His lifestyle would surely be pleasing to God. Yet, he is having a very difficult time of it. He is tempted to give up. He can no longer see the point of leading a godly life when those who are ungodly seem to be prospering. Everything seems to be going wrong for him and nothing is going right. He knows plague and punishment all day long.

To make matters worse and cause him yet more grief and distress, he looked around at the ungodly and what does he see? He describes for us the successful man (or woman) who has it made and has everything going for him or her. This is someone who has become prosperous and has much wealth. She has no troubles or difficulties in her life. She is proud and arrogant.

---

[63] Psalm 73:2

We can see how relevant and up to date these words are. For we see many around us today who are very successful, as far as the world is concerned. They say, "we have no time for God and yet, look how well we are doing without Him. Look at you. Look how much trouble and how many problems you have, and you say you are godly and believe in God!"

Sounds familiar, doesn't it?

Asaph believed in a holy, righteous, true God who intervenes on behalf of His people, loving them and fulfilling His promises to them. How could he and how can we reconcile this with what we see happening to the ungodly who appear to do so well?

The first important lesson for us to learn here concerns the nature of God as God:

> *"For my thoughts are not your thoughts,*
> *neither are your ways my ways,"*
> *declares the LORD.*
> *"As the heavens are higher than the earth,*
> *so are my ways higher than your ways*
> *and my thoughts than your thoughts.*

God's thoughts and ways are not our thoughts and ways, and so it should not surprise us if we do not understand what God chooses to do. His ways are eternal and infinitely above our ways.

The psalmist admits in the third verse that he was envious of the foolish and the arrogant. He who had been so richly blessed by God envied the ungodly he saw around him.

> *For I envied the arrogant*
> *when I saw the prosperity of the wicked.*

And what of us? Do we do the same?

In the very first verse, we have the conclusion that the psalmist comes to. He comes to realise that God is always good to Israel, to those who are really concerned about pleasing Him.

> *Surely God is good to Israel,*
> *to those who are pure in heart.*

So how then does he get from a position where his feet were slipping, back to that strong position of faith which is certain and unshakable?

As we move through the psalm, we see that the writer is beginning to move towards uttering blasphemous thoughts. He is still perplexed about the way he feels he is being treated by God and by the way he feels God is dealing with him. His heart and mind are in turmoil and he thinks he has an awful problem to deal with.

He feels like this until he begins to see those people he had envied as they really are and as they really stand before a holy God.

And now we come to the crux of the matter.

In verse 17 the psalmist enters the sanctuary of God:

In the sanctuary of God things begin to become clear to him. He is put right in his thinking, and he begins to gradually climb out of his despair and his doubting and move from thinking blasphemous thoughts to that wonderful position of knowing with all certainty that "*God is always good to Israel*" as we saw in the first verse.

The second vital lesson for us to learn here is that it is absolutely essential for us **to think spiritually**.

> ..... *I entered the sanctuary of God;*
> *then I understood their final destiny.*

Let me explain what I mean by this.

Up to this point in the psalm, the writer had been dealing with his problem solely relying on his own understanding and his own thoughts. He had been reasoning in a human way, if you like, and this had not helped him at all.

This is how he was thinking: The godly, those in which he includes himself, are suffering while the ungodly are prospering, so where is God in all of this? We see the psalmist going around in circles getting nowhere, because he is thinking in a human way and is not thinking spiritually.

It is very important for us as Christians to guard against slipping back into worldly thinking. When we become Christians, we begin to think in a different way, in a spiritual way. When something happens to us that we do not understand, the moment we begin to feel resentful towards God, the moment we complain that what is happening to us is not fair, then we are bringing God down to our level of understanding. We must instead look at everything from a spiritual perspective. We must learn to think in a spiritual way, particularly with the whole problem of understanding God's ways with us.

When I tried to understand all this,
it was oppressive to me
till I entered the sanctuary of God;
then I understood their final destiny.[64]

So, the Psalmist went into God's sanctuary and he began to think in a right way. But that was just the beginning. He was given understanding and so, he was able to find a solution to his problem.

What was it he began to understand? He understood their end. He understood their final destiny.

This is the thing he had totally forgotten about! His thinking was incomplete, and he only saw things from one viewpoint. But once he went into God's house, he was able to see the whole picture.

He began to see that the position of the ungodly is precarious and dangerous.

Surely you place them on slippery ground;
you cast them down to ruin.[65]

Everything they value so highly is temporary but in their sinful state they are blind to this fact. As he realises the truth of their position, far from envying them, the psalmist might even have begun to feel sorry for them.

So should it be for us. We should be compassionate and show concern for those "dead in trespasses and sins".[66]

His thinking about God was all wrong before he entered the temple. He had been questioning God.

When we doubt God's character, we then doubt God's power. Often people ask, do they not, if God is powerful, why does He allow this or that to happen in the world? The psalmist reminds himself and us of God's power and reminds us that God is in control:

Surely you place them on slippery ground;
you cast them down to ruin.[67]

Nothing is outside the control of God. There is no limit to God's power. The Lord reigns. The psalmist needs to be reminded of this and so do we. He knows that God is faithful and that there are

[64] Psalm 73:16-17
[65] Psalm 73:18
[66] Ephesians 2:1
[67] Psalm 73:18

promises in the Scriptures which can never be broken. What He says, He will do. His promises are to His chosen people, those who are loved by God, protected and blessed by Him.

In the sanctuary, the psalmist's attitude has now changed. He no longer asks why he is treated in this way, but he recognises that God **is** always good to Israel, even when things may appear to the contrary.

Now inside God's house and thinking spiritually, he sees himself as the truly wretched man that he is. Instead of feeling hard done by and sorry for himself, Asaph stops to take a long hard look at himself and sees his need of repentance.

Surely this is something needed among Christians today, as so often we become comfortable in our Christian life.

After Asaph has entered the sanctuary of God and considered his situation from God's perspective, we find him beginning to come up out of the depths of his despair. Having realised his own wretchedness, he now sees himself as always in the presence of God and he is amazed.

> *Yet I am always with you;*
> *you hold me by my right hand.*
> *You guide me with your counsel,*
> *and afterwards you will take me into glory.*[68]

Now he asks a different kind of question.

Why has God not cast him aside as being unworthy?

Well, the Bible tells us the answer to that question. It is because of God's grace.

This is the great message of the psalm to us – it shows us the amazing grace which God has bestowed on those who put their trust in Him, through the saving work of the Lord Jesus Christ.

Despite all our faults and failings, He has forgiven us, He loves us, and we are continually in His presence. It was God who had kept the psalmist's feet from slipping and losing a foothold. So it should be with us. When we stumble and slip, when we fall into sin, God will hold us in His mighty hand and not let us go.

---

[68] Psalm 73:23-24

In the last few verses of the psalm, we see the writer turn to the future as God has restored him with the express purpose of keeping him for glory.

As Asaph moves on in his thinking he is able to tell us that when things have gone wrong, when he is really at the end of his tether, when he doesn't know where to go or to whom to turn, when he needed comfort and solace and strength and reassurance, he has found that there is no-one but God to help and meet his needs.

Whom have I in heaven but you?
And earth has nothing I desire besides you.

His life was empty when he moved away from God. He could find no satisfaction in other things or other places. He had tried what the world had to offer and found it did not fulfil his needs. He now desires God more than the things that God gives. He desires nothing in heaven or on earth but God.

What are you looking for and hoping for in heaven? Do you look forward to being in heaven? We are never told in Scripture to look forward to death ,but very frequently told we are to look forward to heaven and to seeing God.

As Asaph's physical health becomes poor, as he becomes frail and weak in old age, in verse 26, he again is encouraged as he knows that God is the source of his strength forever. So it will be for us. God will sustain us and be our rock.

I trust that all who read this book will consider again carefully the final words of the psalm and come, in saving faith, to the God of the psalmist and the One who will be your God too if you make Him your Sovereign Lord and refuge.

Those who are far from you will perish;
you destroy all who are unfaithful to you.
But as for me, it is good to be near God.
I have made the Sovereign LORD my refuge;
I will tell of all your deeds.[69]

---

[69] Psalm 73:27-28

10

Trust in the LORD

I think I can safely say that each and every one of us will have experienced some difficulties, some trials and some troubles in our life.

Perhaps we have or have had concerns about family members; perhaps we have had financial difficulties and money worries; it's very likely that we have had some illness, maybe even serious and we will have been touched by bereavement and the loss of a loved one.

Often problems come suddenly when we least expect them, and they can lead to a real time of testing of our faith. How do those of us who are Christians cope in such times of testing?

In June 2012, I was diagnosed with breast cancer. It was unexpected and was discovered following a routine mammogram which, like many women, I had had done and walked away from without giving it another thought. So, it came as a shock when I was called for a second mammogram and the subsequent diagnosis was made.

At that time, my husband and I had plans in place as we settled into our retirement. We were both just completing the first year of a ministry training course and had provisionally applied for the second year. Our daughter had just discovered she was expecting another baby and we were looking forward to spending time with our grandchild, once he was born.

We can have our plans, can't we? But sometimes the Lord has different plans for our life. How were we going to cope in this new situation? What were the Lord's plans for us now?

Well, in God's grace and mercy and love for us, He brought to our attention many Scriptures at that time to encourage us and enable us to turn to Him in what was a very real time of need. I say us, as my husband and I were very much together in this although there were of course things I had to do without him. What amazed us was that the Scripture verse that was given changed according to our need.

So, when for example, I had the diagnosis, the Lord gave one verse. And later on, when I had to face surgery in hospital, He gave a different verse. And each time the verse or verses were absolutely apt and were exactly what was needed at that particular moment.

Right at the beginning, the Lord drew my attention to the verses that this chapter is about. These are verses which many readers will know well, I'm sure, and were verses that were very familiar to me.

But sometimes, perhaps, we have to learn that a verse we know very well, that trots off the tongue quite glibly, has to be relearnt and looked at again in a fresh new way. And that's what happened to me where these verses were concerned. For in times of suffering the Lord wants to teach us and He does so through His word.

The verses that the Lord laid on my heart particularly were found in the book of Proverbs:

> *Trust in the Lord with all your heart*
> *and lean not on your own understanding;*
> *in all your ways acknowledge Him*
> *and He will make your paths straight.*[70]

Let's unpack these words and look at them more closely.

First of all, we have the word "trust."

What exactly is trust? To trust is to lean on or rely on someone or something.

Let us think for a moment of an example. A small child is crossing a busy road with a parent. The child puts his hand in the hand of the parent and crosses the road fully trusting that his father or mother will care for him and do everything possible to keep him safe while crossing the road. The child does not fret and worry about the traffic but relies completely on his parent. This is a very important lesson we have to learn as Christians.

So, we are to trust. But in whom or in what are we trust?

The verse gives us the answer. ......

We are to trust **in the Lord**.

Can I ask you, who or what are you trusting in?

[70] Proverbs 3:5-6

During my journey with breast cancer, I met lots of women as you can imagine, travelling the same journey, most of whom were not Christians. In whom or what was their trust? Well, for many, their trust was 100% in their doctor, their oncologist or their nurse who was looking after them.

For others, their trust was 100% in the tablets, the medication they had been given.

But that's not how it must be for us, if we are Christians.

Now, please don't get me wrong. These things are of course very helpful, and the Lord uses them, and we can be grateful to Him for the skills and knowledge of such medical staff and for the medical advancements that have been made, even in our lifetime.

But our trust, the verse tells us, is to be in the Lord, not in anyone or anything else.

First of all, of course, there must be faith in the Lord and then we must put our trust in a person- in God Himself.

So it seems right to ask at this point the question, "Who is this person in whom we are called on, to put our trust?

Going back to our illustration of a child, we would only encourage our children or grandchildren to trust someone they knew, who was known to be trustworthy, would we not?

What then can we draw from the Scriptures to help us answer this question? We turn to Psalm 18:

> The LORD is my rock, my fortress and my deliverer;
> my God is my rock, in whom I take refuge.[71]

David gives us the answer to our question in this psalm. He paints a portrait of God, if you like, and shows us who God is.

Firstly, He is our rock – a firm foundation on which we can stand and feel secure.

Secondly, He is our fortress – a safe shelter in which we can hide and find protection.

Thirdly, He is our deliverer – when all seems hopeless and we have no answers, God comes alongside us and sets us free.

[71] Psalm 18:2

Fourthly, He is our God – how amazing that we can say that. He is faithful, unchanging and perfect. He knows everything, sees everything and is sovereign over everything.

And finally, He is our strength – we who are weak and vulnerable have a source of power and confidence.

All of this is available to us if we put our trust in the Lord. Is He not most certainly trustworthy?

So, we return to our verse in Proverbs. We have learnt that we are to trust, we are to trust the Lord and now we can go further for the verse continues,

Trust in the Lord with all your heart.[72]

Do you remember how I said at the beginning of this chapter that sometimes we have to relearn a verse?

This is the part of the verse I had to look at in a fresh way. This is how previously I would have read the verse, "Trust in the Lord with all your heart."

There is a word in that verse I had to learn and it is that little word "all".

It was as though the Lord was telling me to read the verse like this:

*Trust in the Lord with **ALL** your heart.*

Can you see the difference? The emphasis is now firmly on the word "all". The Lord was showing me that I needed to trust Him with ALL my heart.

It was as though the Lord was asking, "Do you trust Me **wholeheartedly?** Do you trust Me in the midst of this disease and all that it entails?"

That's what He wants all of us to do, doesn't He? Not trust Him in some things, some of the time but in all things all of the time. This is very challenging for all of us.

So, how do we go about trusting the Lord with all our heart?

I'm going to suggest three ways in which we should trust in the Lord and each way begins with the letter 'E'.

The first way is to trust God **entirely** with all our heart.

God demands an undivided commitment to Himself. Too often, the nation of Israel had a divided loyalty between the Lord and the

---

[72] Proverbs 3:5-6

false gods of the nations. We can be tempted to trust the wisdom of the world rather than rely upon divine revelation.

Are you looking for clearer direction in a specific matter? Are you having trouble making a decision? Are you worried about the future?

These words from Proverbs give us good counsel. Do what you can do but leave the results to God. Don't be anxious but put your trust in the Lord. Remember, worry can't do anything, but God can do everything when we put our trust in Him.

First, then, we have to trust. Secondly, we are told "not to lean on our own understanding".

We are to lean on Christ, not on ourselves or our own understanding in any given situation. We all experience in life things we don't understand as I did in the summer of 2012. We don't understand what is happening to us and we certainly don't understand why.

The danger is, of course, that we do lean on our own understanding and as we do so we miss God's will for our life. This proverbial warning is not suggesting that Christians turn off their brains and ignore their own intelligence and common sense. Not at all. It is simply cautioning us not to depend on our own wisdom and experience or indeed that of others. When we become wise in our own eyes we are certainly heading for trouble.

If you can't figure something out, don't try to. God can see everything, including our future. Lean on His understanding for He understands all things. We can thank the Lord that we don't **have** to figure things out on our own. Sometimes life feels so out of control and we are not sure what we should do next. In the world in which we live the advice we so often hear is that we should be self-sufficient but, as Christians, we know that doesn't really work. When we fail to consult God, we tend to mess things up.

The second way we are to trust God is to trust Him **exclusively.**

We are not to lean on our own understanding. The wise person does not rely on her own inclinations and desires, but trusts that God's way is best. As God's children, our place is not to try to understand but to trust.

Let us think of Job for a moment.

In the midst of all his tremendous suffering, Job recognised this. He didn't understand what was happening to him or why. Yet he was able to say these words, "Though He (that is, God) slay me, yet will I trust Him."

Whatever afflictions come into our life, we are to trust God and believe

➤ that He is in control;
➤ that He has our best interests at heart;
➤ that He will never allow us to face more than we can handle and
➤ that He has already secured complete and lasting victory over evil through the Lord Jesus Christ.

As we move on to the second part of the words from Proverbs that were laid on my heart, we encounter that little word "all" again. It may be little, but it demands a lot of us.

In all your ways acknowledge Him.....[73]

Here we have our third 'e' word for we are to trust God **extensively.**

Whether large or small, we are to look to God in all things. We are not merely to acknowledge God's Lordship in our religious life but over every aspect of our life. We must acknowledge that He is Lord in our family life, in our jobs, our friendships and with our finances. He is Lord of all or not Lord at all and we must recognise His Lordship in the small things as well as the great things of life.

What does this mean exactly?

The phrase "acknowledge Him" seems to suggest recognising God for who He is, being aware of God, having fellowship with Him. We are to let Him have complete control. We are to recognise what God has already done for us and what He can do for us.

Let's look at an example to illustrate this: If we were to cultivate only part of our garden and leave the rest, it won't be long before the weeds take over the cultivated area.

It is the same for us in a way. We must try not to keep part of our life to ourselves.

[73] Proverbs 3:6

88

I wonder, is anyone trying to do that? Do we try to be one thing in church and something different when in the world? We must guard against this. The challenge to all of us is to acknowledge the Lord in **all** things.

And so, we come to the final words of the verses we are considering in this chapter as we seek to see what they say about trusting God.

Verse 6 is so uplifting and encouraging. We can consider what it says from two slightly different translations of the Bible.

The New King James Version[74] reads: *And He shall direct your paths*. The New International Version translates these same words as *He will make your paths straight*.

Here we now have the wonderful promise of guidance and blessing, which follows from doing all the things that have been set out before us.

He will make your paths straight.

The Romans were famous for building straight roads. There is nothing quite like a straight road if your aim is to get to your destination. It's always easier to get on with your journey if the road is straight and there are no turnings to navigate.

What does that mean for us? God will bless those who trust Him. It is a promise of God's leading us all the way to heaven, our final goal, our final destination.

He will direct your paths.

Again, we are given a promise of guidance. God will lead us, so we are on the path that leads us to life and ultimately to heaven itself.

We all need this guidance in our life, do we not? We can thank God that we can turn to Him in faith at any time and seek guidance. He is more than delighted to teach us, to enlighten us, and lead us in the way that we should go. If we put our trust in Him, He promises that He **will** direct our paths.

It is helpful at this point to link these verses in Proverbs with some words in the Psalms:

---

[74] The Holy Bible, New King James Version, Copyright © 1979, 1980, 1982, 1992 Thomas Nelson, Inc.

He (that is a righteous man or woman) will have no fear of
bad news;
his (or her) heart is steadfast, trusting in the LORD.
His (or her) heart is secure; he (or she) will have no fear; ... [75]

Because we live in a fallen world, bad things can and do happen to all of us. We never know, from moment to moment, when devastating news or circumstances may hit without warning. And then there are those situations in which we wait with dread, wondering whether the outcome will be favourable or take a turn for the worse.

The words from the Psalms quoted above tell us that those who have placed their trust wholeheartedly in the Lord will remain steadfast when these things do occur. It is when we rely completely on God that we will not find ourselves shaken. It is when we are fully confident in God's ability to sustain us that a change in our circumstances will not change our poise or throw us off course.

Someone may be thinking, "Well that's easy to say but how can I possibly do that?"

This strength to stand strong comes not from within us but from our Heavenly Father. It comes from our trust in what He can do, not what we can do.

Are you afraid? God is greater than the worst thing that can happen to you. Determine in your heart to trust Him, no matter what comes your way.

You see, fear and trust cannot co-exist at the same time in our hearts. When confronted with fear, we need to make a deliberate choice to be courageous and not to be afraid.

Why? Listen to God speaking to Joshua following the death of Moses.

Notice how powerful the words are. They are a command, not a mild suggestion that we might like to try!

"Be strong and courageous, because you will lead these
people to inherit the land I swore to their forefathers to give
them. Be strong and very courageous. Be careful to obey all
the law my servant Moses gave you; do not turn from it to the
right or to the left, that you may be successful wherever you

---

[75] Psalm 112:7-8

go. Do not let this Book of the Law depart from your mouth;
meditate on it day and night, so that you may be careful to do
everything written in it. Then you will be prosperous and
successful. Have I not commanded you? Be strong and
courageous. Do not be terrified; do not be discouraged, for
the LORD your God will be with you wherever you go. "[76]

God is on your side and victory is assured. Don't give fear a foothold in your heart. Surrender it immediately to God and turn your thoughts to what God is capable of doing. When we replace fear with trust, we will know that inner peace that comes from resting in God's care and strength.

May the Lord enable each of us to trust Him in these three ways:

➤ entirely,
➤ exclusively,
➤ extensively

and in doing so, may we bring glory and honour to His Name.

[76] Joshua 1:6-9

11

The Purpose of Life

The book of Ecclesiastes, which means "The Preacher", was written about 3000 years ago and yet it has been included in the Bible. We must therefore conclude that it is there for us to read, for a reason and it must not be ignored.

Its message is a timely one and a lasting one, suited to our 21st century world where we live in such secular times. The message of the book is plain. It tells us what kind of living is purposeful and worthwhile.

Throughout the book, Solomon, its author, looks at life from two points of view. He looks at each aspect from one position and then from the opposing position.

Firstly, he views life through the eyes of the unconverted person who lives life without God and tackles whatever life brings without reference to God or His word.

Right at the outset of the book, we see that this way of life is a waste of time.

> "Meaningless! Meaningless!"
> says the Teacher.
> "Utterly meaningless!
> Everything is meaningless."[77]

Secondly, he looks through the eyes of the person who knows God. For the believer who worships and serves God, life has meaning and purpose. It is full of assurance and hope. The life under the sun is contrasted with the life under God, the Maker of that sun.

The first 11 verses serve as an introduction to the book.

We learn that King Solomon is the writer and he also calls himself the preacher to or teacher of the people.

[77] Ecclesiastes 1:2

As Solomon looks at life, he decides that it is a waste of time. It has no point or purpose to it. Everything is only temporary and does not last. He wonders what point there is in our earthly work. However much we succeed in life, however many possessions we acquire, we will end up with nothing, so what is the point of all the effort?

In the gospel of Luke, we read the parable told by Jesus of the rich fool. He was one who had stored up much for many years to come.

But God says to him,

> …… *'You fool! This very night your life will be demanded from you. Then who will get what you have prepared for yourself?'*[78]

We see a similar vein running through Psalm 49 where we read these sobering words:

> *For all can see that wise men die;*
> *the foolish and the senseless alike perish*
> *and leave their wealth to others.*
> *Their tombs will remain their houses for ever,*
> *their dwellings for endless generations,*
> *though they had named lands after themselves.*[79]

Back in chapter 1 of Ecclesiastes, we see Solomon recognizing that every one of us lives for a relatively short time and then dies. One generation follows another.

The writer Shakespeare realized this some 400 or so years ago and gave expression to his thoughts in words spoken by Jacques in his *As You Like It:*

> All the world's a stage,
> And all the men and women merely players;
> They have their exits and their entrances;
> And one man in his time plays many parts,
> His acts being seven ages. At first the infant,
> Mewling and puking in the nurse's arms;
> And then the whining school-boy, with his satchel
> And shining morning face, creeping like snail
> Unwillingly to school. And then the lover,
> Sighing like furnace, with a woeful ballad

---

[78] Luke 12:20
[79] Psalm 49:10-11

Made to his mistress' eyebrow. Then a soldier,
Full of strange oaths, and bearded like the pard,
Jealous in honour, sudden and quick in quarrel,
Seeking the bubble reputation
Even in the cannon's mouth. And then the justice,
In fair round belly with good capon lin'd,
With eyes severe and beard of formal cut,
Full of wise saws and modern instances;
And so he plays his part. The sixth age shifts
Into the lean and slipper'd pantaloon,
With spectacles on nose and pouch on side;
His youthful hose, well sav'd, a world too wide
For his shrunk shank; and his big manly voice,
Turning again toward childish treble, pipes
And whistles in his sound. Last scene of all,
That ends this strange eventful history,
Is second childishness and mere oblivion;
Sans teeth, sans eyes, sans taste, sans everything.[80]

Verses 5 to 7 of Ecclesiastes chapter 1 describe what I've called "The treadmill effect".

Everything goes on in the world as it always has done but nothing actually gets anywhere. The sun rises and sets but has to rise again, the wind blows and comes back to where it started, and the rivers run into the sea but never fill it. Lots of activity is always going on but no real progress is ever made.

Verse 8 describes the frustration and the repetition of life. No matter what our eyes see, or our ears hear they are never satisfied.

And we see from verses 9 and 10 that even history itself tells us how repetitive life is and that there is nothing new on earth.

How often do we say that the same things come around and have been done before? Fashions, conflicts between nations, ideas in education, hair styles. So many things come around again, but they have all been seen before.

If we ever think we are going to make a lasting mark in history we

[80] William Shakespeare, *As You Like It,* Acts 2, Scene 7, lines 139-167

are mistaken. For any impression we make has already been made by others and soon forgotten. Anything we do achieve will soon be forgotten and we will even soon be forgotten by future generations.

We must face up to the fact that there is no such thing as a lasting accomplishment and everything that is done is fundamentally pointless, purposeless and frustrating.

This is life as Solomon saw it from an earthly or human point of view. And he is certainly not alone in seeing life in this way. Very many ordinary people think of life like this and sadly we know that some see life as so futile and such a waste of time that they choose to end it.

What a very depressing picture has been painted for us so far. Perhaps someone is already wishing they had skipped this chapter all together. Perhaps you might be thinking that you were in need of cheering up, not of reading such a solemn, miserable message.

I hope you will continue reading to the end and will soon begin to see from Scripture that things can be very different from this gloomy introduction. Surely there must be more to life than this!

As we look into the next few chapters of Ecclesiastes, we will see what is said to be the key to life.

The last section of chapter 1 gives us an insight into how Solomon was thinking as he tells us he has considered everything *under the sun* in his quest to find purpose and meaning in life.

In these verses Solomon tells us in detail what things under the sun are definitely **not** the key to life and in all he comes to 4 conclusions:

Firstly, Solomon discovers that a search after knowledge and wisdom does not bring with it the fulfilment that he longs for.

Verse 16 tells us that Solomon was indeed a very wise, intellectual man, more than any other man who had lived. Yet he learnt that when a man becomes wise, he finds there is no real point to that wisdom and so he becomes filled with grief and disappointment. He thus concludes that acquiring knowledge and being very intellectual is **not** the key to life.

Secondly, we discover in chapter 2 that Solomon comes to the conclusion that pleasures in life do not completely satisfy. People today are trying to find some sort of fulfilment in pleasure, and leisure activities are pursued more than at any time in history, but the question must be asked "Are they any happier?"

Solomon tried many sorts of pleasures to see if any would last. They brought him short-term happiness and fulfilment, but none really lasted. He went after merriment, drunkenness, and foolishness. He denied himself nothing. He acquired many expensive possessions and land. Because of who he was, Solomon was able to have whatever he wanted without counting the cost.

Yet after doing all this, he found that life was still futile and a waste of time.

How many people today spend a lifetime accumulating wealth and possessions, only to discover an empty void inside which none of these things can fill?

So, like Solomon, we too must conclude that spending our life enjoying ourselves is **not** the key to life.

Thirdly, again in chapter 2 we learn that holding a pre-eminent position does not bring the satisfaction you might expect it to bring.

Solomon knew that his was a position of pre-eminence, of superiority over other men. He was greater in every respect than they were. He was wiser than those he saw around him and he saw many who were fools. Yet he tells us that ultimately what happens to the foolish person also happens to the wise one.

So, argues Solomon, what is the point in being wise if you end up the same as the foolish?

What is the point of being "the king pin", excelling above others in work or sport or whatever else you spent your time pursuing? According to Solomon there is no point at all. So, Solomon again concludes that pre-eminence is not the key to life.

Today many people try to find a purpose in their lives, they try to find fulfilment through fame and fortune. It is not long before they realise that they still feel empty inside and yearn for something more which they are unable to find in earthly things.

Many people say that life will be so very different and so much better for them if only they had more money, or a bigger house or a better car or promotion in their job or more holidays or shorter working hours. Yet many who acquire these things testify to the fact that they did not bring the satisfaction they wanted or expected to get from them.

And finally, in our list of negatives, Solomon concludes that hard work is not the key to life.

Staying in chapter 2 we learn that he spent much of his time building and investing for the future. Solomon even sees the labour of his own hands as futile and a waste of time. Everything we work for is ultimately left behind to someone else.

Solomon had behaved wisely but bemoans the fact that the one who comes after him may not be so wise and may even be a fool. The one who will inherit Solomon's wealth will not have worked down through the years for any of the things that will be left to him. Solomon looks back at all he has achieved, and he is filled with despair. He wonders whether it was all worth the effort and the hard work.

Verses 21 to 23 make us consider what we have got out of working hard when we realise that we will leave everything we have worked for to someone else who may not deserve it and will not have earned it. We may lose sleep worrying at night about our business or the amount of work we have to do, but at the end of the day, what good does it really do us?

So then, where does all of this leave us?

Where is lasting satisfaction and fulfilment to be found?

It is not to be found in education, nor is it found in being on the top rung of the business ladder. It is not in material possessions, nor in working hard. It is not even in being the king with all his wealth and position.

No, it is not in any of these things.

Now we move at last to the positive and we see from chapter 2 verse 24 to chapter 3 verse 15 how we **can** have a life with purpose and value. God is now being brought into things. God is now in the picture.

Solomon now begins to look at things from the other side of the coin, as it were, from the viewpoint of someone who has God in his life, and he now comes to 3 very different conclusions.

Firstly, he discovers that satisfaction in life is possible with God. It is a gift given by God.

> *To the man who pleases him, God gives wisdom, knowledge*
> *and happiness, ...*[81]

It is the person who leaves God out of their life that lives a futile existence. Ultimately everything the sinner does works out for the benefit of those who are in God's favour.

> *..... but to the sinner he gives the task of gathering and storing*
> *up wealth to hand it over to the one who pleases God.*[82]

What a staggering thought that is!

Don't be too keen to envy those you know who seem to be faring better than you. Solomon is quite clear in these verses: once God is in our lives, once God is in the picture, life takes on a meaning and purpose it otherwise would not have.

Secondly, we learn that everything is planned. As Solomon looks at life again through the eyes of God, he sees that everything is part of a great plan and that there is a time for everything.

> *There is a time for everything,*
> *and a season for every activity under heaven:*
> *a time to be born and a time to die,*
> *a time to plant and a time to uproot,*
> *a time to kill and a time to heal,*
> *a time to tear down and a time to build,*
> *a time to weep and a time to laugh,*
> *a time to mourn and a time to dance,*
> *a time to scatter stones and a time to gather them,*
> *a time to embrace and a time to refrain,*
> *a time to search and a time to give up,*
> *a time to keep and a time to throw away,*
> *a time to tear and a time to mend,*
> *a time to be silent and a time to speak,*
> *a time to love and a time to hate,*
> *a time for war and a time for peace.*[83]

There is an appointed time for everything that happens in this world of ours. Nothing happens by chance but is part of the divine

---

[81] Ecclesiastes 2:26a
[82] Ecclesiastes 2:26b
[83] Ecclesiastes 3:1-8

scheme. Everything that occurs has an overall purpose, therefore, which is part of God's eternal plan.

Where the non-Christian might ask, "What is the point of it all?" the believer now sees that there is a point to everything. She knows that all things work together for good, as the apostle Paul reminds us in Romans chapter 8.

Thirdly and finally, Solomon comes to see that everything is full of purpose. From chapter 3 verses 9 to 15, we see that what **we** do soon passes but whatever God does lasts forever. **His** work never has anything wrong with it or needs any improvement. God is working out His purpose in all things in the world and He desires that we should fear Him.

Verse 15 speaks of a seemingly endless cycle of repetition of what has already been. But when we realise it is God who controls this cycle, we see that nothing is pointless because everything serves His purpose and is under His direction.

The book of Ecclesiastes is a very 21st century book and its teaching is bang up to date. Many people feel undervalued in their place of work and their efforts don't seem to matter. The suicide rate among young men is at an all-time high. The call for euthanasia becomes ever louder as more and more people see no point in life and want to have the right to end it.

But once we realise that there is a God and all things are in His hands, then everything takes on a new significance and a new perspective. We can rest content in the knowledge that He will work out all things according to His plan and purpose.

From an earthly perspective Solomon concluded that everything in this life was pointless and insignificant but as he looked at life from God's point of view, as it were, he saw that everything was part of a grand plan. There is a season, an appointed time, for every event that takes place. Every detail in life has a purpose and is tied into that eternal plan.

What we do does soon pass. It is what God does that lasts forever.

It is important for each and every one of us to realise that we are all faced with a choice in how we live our life, short though that may be. We must either live a life of untold frustration or we must live in the fear of the Lord.

I trust that each one reading this will have a purpose in life through knowing the Lord and resting in the knowledge that He is working out His eternal plan, day by day.

12

A Message from the Prophet Amos

Amos was a farmer living in the village of Tekoa, about 10 miles from Jerusalem. He prophesied about 750BC and was called to declare God's will to the people of Israel. Things had gone from bad to worse as far as the nation of Israel was concerned. At that time a minority of Israelites, mainly the nation's leaders, were wealthy and were full of greed for more. Money was one of their gods but many of the ordinary people were poor and were badly treated, the nation had become immoral in their daily living and worst of all in God's sight was the false religion that had taken over the nation. Altars and idols such as golden calves had been built and Baal worship had crept into Israel's worship.

We can see parallels in our own day. For many years we have seen a "going to church" mentality perhaps at Christmas or Easter but in recent years even that has declined. There is little true commitment to the Lord Jesus Christ or His Word.

As a result, standards of morality and other Christian values have fallen as the nation rejects God and His ways for us to live. As a nation and as individuals we are prosperous and yet further away from God than we were when we were materially poorer.

The message of Amos speaks to us all about things that truly matter – righteousness, justice, and our eternal destiny, our relationship to a holy God, judgment and salvation.

Israel was the church in the Old Testament. She had been given God's word to guide the people and His presence was with them, yet she rejected Him. Israel had entered into a covenant relationship with God yet became careless about the things of God. The warning to present day Christians is clear. The prophecy contains a warning for those who would deceive themselves into thinking they are Christians, or thinking they are right with God.

And verses in Matthew's gospel carry a similar warning:

"Not everyone who says to me, 'Lord, Lord,' will enter the kingdom of heaven, but only he who does the will of my Father who is in heaven. [22] Many will say to me on that day, 'Lord, Lord, did we not prophesy in your name, and in your name drive out demons and perform many miracles?' [23] Then I will tell them plainly, 'I never knew you. Away from me, you evildoers!' .....[84]

We see the ultimate goal of Amos' s prophecy is to restore Israel back to God for He is the great Deliverer and the One whose desire is to save His people from their sins.

The first two verses give us an introduction to the prophecy.

The words of Amos, one of the shepherds of Tekoa—what he saw concerning Israel two years before the earthquake, when Uzziah was king of Judah and Jeroboam son of Jehoash was king of Israel.

He said:

"The LORD roars from Zion
and thunders from Jerusalem;
the pastures of the shepherds dry up,
and the top of Carmel withers. "[85]

Amos announces God's judgment to come.

God sends the prophet into a society riddled with evil, one that loves pleasure, loves money and is self-centred. Have you heard that somewhere before? He is sent to tell men and women the truth about themselves. He is sent to tell them of their sinfulness and the anger of God as a result of the way they are living.

And to tell them of God's judgment that will surely come to a people who go on rejecting God. For God is not mocked. Oh, men and women love to laugh if told of hell, judgment and punishment. But the very first verse of the prophecy tells us that Amos saw the impending punishment in the form of an earthquake two years before it happened.

So often we are reminded of God's love and grace towards us and

---

[84] Matthew 7:21-23
[85] Amos 1:1-2

how wonderful that is.

This book in Scripture is a timely reminder that God is not one to be trifled with.

Verse 2 tells us that He roars, something we associate with a lion. In chapter 3 we see God showing His righteous indignation, which is His right as the Sovereign Lord. It is the Lord's way of showing that He is not pleased with the wickedness of men and of nations and in particular His own people.

God is sovereign as seen in the way He judges the people. We must remember that He is holy and just. We see the beginning of His judgments when the pastures of the shepherds have dried up; we see that the summit of Mount Carmel has withered, the very place where Elijah was sustained through a drought of three and a half years.

All events in history are in the providence of God. Nations and individuals must beware for, as we read in the letter to the Hebrews,

It is a dreadful thing to fall into the hands of the living God.[86]

So then, the early chapters of Amos clearly set out the judgment that will come on the nations.

But we must remember that the book of Amos is not just about doom and gloom. It points us to the saving grace of God, through what we now know to be the redeeming work of the Lord Jesus Christ.

Two aspects of the book are prominent throughout: God's judgment and His grace.

However, it is important to consider the words

This is what the LORD says:
"For three sins ... ...,
even for four, I will not turn back my wrath.[87]

which recur throughout chapter 1 and 2 and tell us that there does come a time when God will take only so much of human sin and will no longer seek to turn men and women back to Himself. There will be a day of reckoning and God's perfect justice will be seen. He is slow to anger and holds back His judgment because He is merciful.

Many use the slowness of God in coming in judgment as proof that there is no God. Because they think God does not act, they go on

---

[86] Hebrews 10:31
[87] Amos 1:3b

sinning. But there will come a day when all will see God's justice. We must make sure we are ready for that day.

These verses in Amos teach us something of God's dealings with the world, for the nations are judged in terms of their relationship to God's people. God's anger towards each nation is seen as they are consumed one by one. They are punished according to their sins.

So far Amos has been talking about "them" and not "us". Those in Israel who heard his message must have thought he was a wonderful preacher. He certainly scored his quota of brownie points with his listeners. All these nations that had been such a trouble to Israel for hundreds of years were now said to be under God's judgement.

Well done, Amos! What an encouraging word and what a clever way to get his audience to listen!

But wait a minute. What is being said in chapter 2 from verse 6 onwards?

Amos does not stop with the nations. In these verses, he is now speaking about the judgment that is to come upon God's own people, Israel, rather than the ungodly nations round about.

Now the preacher is not so popular!

Look at these striking words:

"You only have I chosen
of all the families of the earth;
therefore, I will punish you
for all your sins."[88]

Israel had been brought into a place of privilege and responsibility. The people had sinned knowingly, even though God had lavished His special kindness upon them. They had rejected His law and not kept His commandments. They had worshipped false gods. They had been kept by His power throughout many generations and been brought out of slavery in Egypt. They knew the truth and had thrown it in God's face, as it were. Their punishment would be much more severe.

So, what exactly are the sins of Israel that have brought such judgment upon them?

Amos gives us 4 examples.

First of all, the judges were corrupt and could be bought. The rich

---

[88] Amos 3:2

were allowed to oppress the poor and the innocent, and enslave them for having the smallest of debts.

Secondly, they enjoyed seeing the poor in misery. The poor were to be kept in their place.

Thirdly, sexual immorality was widespread.

And fourthly, they showed contempt for what was sacred.

The prophet reminds them of their history, of God's loving presence having been with them down through the years, of the prophets God sent to tell them, and of His grace and salvation.

How had they responded?

When the prophets had shown the people up for what they really were, they were offended by the message brought to them.

When the Lord God brings judgment upon them, their strength, their skill and their speed will not save them or help them to escape.

Amos's warnings of the impending judgments seem most improbable. But within 50 years the kingdom was completely destroyed.

Let's look at some predictions.

First, Israel is particularly accountable because of their privileged position before God. He knew them and had called them in a way that no other nation had been known or called. He had shown them His special favour and showered His love upon them over many generations. They had broken the covenant between God and themselves.

More than this, the surrounding nations were looking on.

Notice the parallels with the church today. Israel should have been a witness to the pagan nations round about, pointing them to the Lord God. Instead, these nations are now witnessing their sinfulness, their decline and God's judgment upon them. Not only that, but the nations themselves are going to be used by God to speak against Israel. Their false religion will be swept away, the rich will lose their posh houses and the symbols of mercy will be smashed. And all of it being watched by the pagan nations.

What a lesson for the church today. The world is watching the church and us, if we are members of it. We are to be salt and light. We are to practice what we preach. We are to walk the talk, as they say.

The world expects us to live lives that are different from theirs. If the life of the Christian is as worldly as the person next door, why should he or she listen when they are told of their need of a Saviour? Our faith must not consist of just a lot of words. As James says, "Faith without works is dead".

Tragically, Israel in the time of Amos pointed the ungodly away from the Lord God. Sadly, much of what is done in the name of Christ today does exactly the same.

What a sobering and challenging thought!

Why should God not act in a similar way towards the church in the west today? Why are many within the church allowed to go on denying the truths of the Bible and end up believing nothing?

God not only used Amos to pronounce judgment but also to call the nation of Israel to repentance. The message is the same today. And it begins first with the church. We must not sit back and be complacent in the security that we get from living in the west. God is merciful but will not stay His hand forever.

Second, the destruction of a pleasure-seeking culture is predicted.

The Israelites had many warnings and had been delivered from many disasters but still did not turn back to God. They refused to see His hand in their affairs and certainly did not repent of their sinful way of life.

Now we see that the final judgement involves meeting God.

Often seen on boards, these words, "Prepare to meet your God", have been laughed at and ridiculed by those who obviously do not believe the truth of them. Yet we see from other parts of scripture that all men and women must one day stand before this same God about whom we have read is roaring from His place on high.

Israel had time to prepare. How well was that time used?

We have time to prepare and must ensure that we use that time wisely and are ready to meet our God. Are we prepared to meet this awesome and almighty God?

Verse 13 reminds us that the One who formed the majestic mountains you see around you, the One who makes the wind blow, the One who turns the day into night and controls the elements, who moves around the earth according to his own plan and purpose is the Lord God Almighty.

Much has been said about judgment. We would be left in a most wretched of states if the book of Amos stopped there.

But as we move to chapter 5, we read of God calling Israel to repentance.

The proclamation of divine judgment on the one hand is seen over and against the heart-felt plea even at this late stage of national history, to repent and turn back to God.

Seek me and live, says the Lord in verse 4.

Seek the Lord and live, is the call, in verse 6.

Seek good, not evil, that you may live, says Amos in verse 14. *Then the Lord God Almighty will be with you, just as you say He is.*[89]

Notice in verse 1 how Amos tells them of their plight through the words of a lament. This is normally associated with death and mourning. It is as though Amos is telling the people to look into their own coffin and see that they are spiritually dead.

A similar message is to be found in Revelation where the church at Sardis is similarly warned.

Of course, it is important to remember that the word of God is living and is written for those who are living. So, what is written in Scripture is appropriate for the church today. In fact, it is vital and essential for the well-being of any church to read the Bible and abide by its teaching.

The paradox continues and we must take heed of it. God's divine judgment, His wrath if we do not listen to what He has to say, is balanced with His mercy, grace and desire for the church to seek Him and live.

Church history is littered with the memorials of congregations and whole denominations that once flourished and are now gone for ever, together with the distinctive doctrines they believed were the unchangeable word of God.

Why did they disappear? No doubt many reasons could be given. It is sometimes said that the young people didn't stay in the church. Or it's a day of small things. Or the members couldn't afford to repair the buildings.

---

[89] Amos 5:14

But what it all came down to, in the end, was that God withdrew His blessing from those churches or denominations.

What about churches that are still apparently alive? After all, the message is for the living, not for the dead.

Well, outwardly Israel was quite prosperous. Many churches today are similarly thriving. There may be a great deal of activity going on, perhaps a wide range of organizations are catering for every age group in the church and the local community, or many meetings may be being held during the week. Perhaps even services are fully attended on Sundays.

Israel may have been dead, from God's point of view, but you would not have said so had you seen numbers attending.

We must therefore look at the deeper things.

As the Lord Jesus Christ said – and Matthew records this in his gospel,

> "Woe to you, teachers of the law and Pharisees, you hypocrites! You give a tenth of your spices—mint, dill and cummin. But you have neglected the more important matters of the law—justice, mercy and faithfulness. You should have practiced the latter, without neglecting the former.[90]

It is important to stress that this message is for the church, not the world outside. Israel was outwardly very religious. The people were very keen on their sacrifices, they gave their tithes and offerings and they kept their own religious observances.

The warning here is not that we fall away from the church into worldliness, but that we follow our own ways in terms of worship and other outward signs into what might be called false religion. The warning is to nominal Christians who try to appease God by their outward religion yet live as they want to live in this life, pleasing themselves not God.

Here the word of God challenges this position.

Chapter 5 predicts the end of false religion.

The Israelites were comfortable with the religious system that they had put in place despite the fact that it was false. It was very different from the religion of Jehovah as portrayed in the word of God and they

---

[90] Matthew 23:23

110

were aware of this. They were not pleased with prophets such as Amos who came to remind them of their sins and tell them how God wanted them to live.

They took part in religious occasions, went to church, gave their offerings and yet at the same time cheated the poor and lived lives of materialism and greed.

They even looked forward to the day of the Lord when the judgments of God would be brought down on their enemies. It is quite amazing that the Israelites saw no danger for themselves in the coming day of the Lord. As far as they were concerned, God was on their side and it never occurred to them that He might be angry with them and their lifestyle.

But is this not like people in many of our churches today? There are church leaders in some churches and pulpits denying the Bible and rejecting what the Bible teaches.

Many scientists tell us that man has outgrown the myths of Genesis. Jesus is nothing but a good teacher, people say. God Himself is just some mysterious being or even something in man's imagination. Yet they, like the Israelites at the time of Amos, cling to a hope of heaven and assume that if such a place exists, they are assured a place. What complacency!

The real hub of the problem, the real offence to God is having the outward form of godliness but denying the power.

In other words, God is not interested in the outward form of religion but looks at the attitude of the heart. Matthew tells us in chapter 15 that God is offended by people who draw near to Him with their lips while their hearts are far from Him. He does not want their feasts, their offerings, or their songs. He wants them to live His way, a way of justice and righteousness. He requires them to live a life of holiness.

Can it be said that

...... *justice [will] roll on like a river,*
righteousness like a never-failing stream[91]

in the modern church? Or in our daily life?

"The evidence of true religion", writes J A Motyer, "is that it

---

[91] Amos 5:24

touches all life with the holiness of obedience to His word and command."[92]

We discover from our reading of chapter 6 that a complacent attitude leads to the end of the pleasure-seeking class.

Amos comes to a complacent people. As far as they are concerned, they have everything they need to be secure in this life and a religion to take care of the next one.

But look at verse 1.

> *Woe to you who are complacent in Zion,*
> *and to you who feel secure on Mount Samaria,*
> *you notable men of the foremost nation,*
> *to whom the people of Israel come!*[93]

Through Amos, God challenges their complacency. He makes them look at the facts. They should look at the nations around them. They are small and insignificant and have little military strength. Of course, Israel could feel strong and confident. but they were fooling themselves if they thought they could defeat the enemy when God raises up a powerful nation against them.

God takes away the two things they are relying on for their security. He takes away their wealth and their power.

Thus, the end of wealth is predicted.

The prophet Amos is not trying to tell us that wealth in and of itself is wrong. In verses 4-7 he is concerned about excess wealth. The leaders in Israel were self-indulgent, they were feasting and drinking while having no regard or concern for the suffering of the poor. Wealth had become their god and he is showing them that this is about to be taken away from them, as they are taken into exile.

Then the end of power is predicted.

The leaders expressed their power through lack of justice in the land and through their military might.

Amos stresses the truth that it is foolish to trust in military power. The Israelites boast about their military achievements when they have really amounted to nothing. And now God is going to send a greater power, Assyria, to defeat them.

---

[92] J. A. Motyer, *The Day of the Lion*, IVP, 1974, p.137
[93] Amos 6:1

Any military power they may think they have will be taken away from them.

As we come to the closing chapter of the prophecy, we see the mood beginning to change. Now there is the promise of a future day of salvation!

Amos begins to look beyond judgment to salvation.

All those sinners in Israel who are complacent and who think judgment does not apply to them will die. But a final note of hope points us again to God's mercy and longsuffering, for we read of the promise of Israel being restored once more.

This is the true security given by the Lord to Israel and to all who believe. The security of heaven is given to us for eternity, if we trust in the Lord Jesus Christ for our salvation and our hope.

This is looking to the future when people from all nations and every corner of the earth will be among the people of God and will share in the privileges only Israel had known. This is pointing us to the coming of the Lord Jesus Christ and His great kingdom, and the offer of salvation that He brings to Jews and Gentiles, to all who would believe.

How is this word written so long ago relevant to us today?

We must not forget the two things that angered God and brought down His judgment on the people. Pleasure-seeking materialism and an outward form of religion were the downfall of Israel.

God does not change. He is the same today as He was in the time of Amos. The two things which angered God then will anger Him today. They will be the downfall of the 21st century church if we do not heed the warning in the book of Amos.

Yet, for those who are trusting Jesus, who know their sins forgiven through His sacrifice on the cross, their hearts will be full of praises to Him and they will seek to lead lives that please Him, knowing that one day they will be eternally secure in His presence.

13

Becoming a Titus 2 Woman

What sort of a woman are you? How would others describe you? Perhaps for some it will be the old or older woman, the thin or not so thin woman, the tall or the short woman. It might be the kind or the helpful woman, the rude or the interfering woman, or the religious, church going woman. You can substitute your own description of yourself. I hope that all who read this chapter will have, or will be determined to have, a new title, the Titus 2 woman.

What is a Titus 2 woman, you might be thinking?

The short answer is an older, mature Christian woman who teaches and encourages the younger women. Her ministry is based on verses from Titus chapter 2.

Paul, writing to young Titus says,

> *Likewise, teach the older women to be reverent in the way they live, not to be slanderers or addicted to much wine, but to teach what is good. [4] Then they can train the younger women to love their husbands and children, [5] to be self-controlled and pure, to be busy at home, to be kind, and to be subject to their husbands, so that no-one will malign the word of God.*[94]

This ministry is something that is lacking in the churches today. It is something that every Christian woman should aspire to be.

Before we look at these verses and their teaching in detail, there are two things which must be stated clearly at the outset.

Firstly, anything we seek to accomplish can only be done by the grace and power of God, not in our own strength.

And secondly, these verses are directed to women who are Christian. So if there is anyone reading this book who as yet has not

---

[94] Titus 2:3-5

committed her life to Christ, then can I urge you to turn to Him, seek forgiveness for your sins and then you can ask Him to teach you from His word that you too might become a Titus 2 woman?

Let's begin to unpack these verses. We see that they give us the pattern we need for godly womanhood.

Verse 3 is addressed to the older women in the church.

Firstly, what sort of person ought the older woman to be, before she can begin to teach others?

It is clear that before we can take on such a role, we must be taught ourselves, and have been dealt with in our own life by the Lord. We have to be in the right place ourselves according to God's word. Before we can begin to disciple or teach young women, we must be a good example to them in our own behaviour and in the way we live our own life. We, as older, experienced godly women are called on here, says Paul, to teach good things to those who are younger.

Obviously, God does not want an older woman to be a bad influence on the younger Christian woman. He wants her to have a godly character. The behaviour of the older woman must always reflect holiness.

So, Paul gives four instructions for older women to follow.

The first instruction is that the older woman should be reverent in the way she lives. What does this mean exactly?

It means she is to behave in a proper manner. She should act and dress in a manner pleasing to God. She should be outwardly different from the world; pure and holy within. She is called away from the ways of the world, where the attitude today is that we live to please ourselves. The Christian woman is to live with an attitude of reverence to God. She loves the Lord, and this must be evident in the way she acts and lives her life.

The second instruction is that she should not be a slanderer. The Christ-like woman is not a malicious gossip. Gossip is a sin, but today as in Paul's day it can often be socially acceptable in a way that other sins are not. It's easy to let out that bit of information about someone else. Sometimes it can make us feel better about ourselves; if we can paint others in a bad light, people may think better of us. The Titus 2 woman guards her words carefully.

We learn here how important it is to be rooted in the Bible and to think Biblically. We are not to be drawn in by the current thinking of the age.

Some time ago, I read a headline in the Daily Mail. It read: "Gossip can be good for you". [95] According to the *Psychological Science Journal*, talking about others and even leaving people out can prevent bullying and encourage co-operation. Furthermore, "reputational information", the new smart name for gossip, can have benefits for society, according to this way of thinking.

No! Gossip or slander is not to be part of the mature Christian woman's way of life!

The third instruction is that the Christian woman is not to be addicted to much wine (or anything else for that matter).

The addicted person is no longer in control of her life but is controlled by her habit. However hard life may become, the godly woman turns to the living God for consolation, not to the bottle or the pot of tablets. If a Christian woman is addicted in this way, she will be of no use at all to younger women and will bring dishonour to the gospel.

Our last instruction is to develop a teaching ministry. The passage says, "Teach what is good".

Paul is here commending the idea that the mature Christian woman should teach and train the younger ones. We will look in detail in a moment at what it is exactly that Scripture requires of us to teach when we come to consider verses 4 and 5.

But in case someone is now gasping in horror at the thought of public speaking, let me hastily say that is not what the verse is necessarily saying.

For some it will include that but not all by any means. The older woman does not have to possess an official gift of teaching. She does not have to speak at women's meetings. No, the older woman is to come alongside a younger woman and encourage her. She can talk with her about the Lord, about the way He has dealt with her, about

---

[95] https://www.dailymail.co.uk/femail/article-2547390/Gossip-GOOD-Talking-leaving-people-prevent-bullying-encourage-cooperation.html accessed 6th April, 2021

His grace in her own life. She can perhaps pray for her and with her and teach what is good.

So back to Verses 4 and 5, quoted above, where we learn what the older women are to teach to the younger women.

Given that the qualities of a mature Christian woman are present in the older woman, then, Paul goes on to tell Titus that they can train the younger women. Verses 4 and 5 serve a dual purpose. They help the older women to understand their responsibility towards the younger women; they also help the younger women to understand what kind of Christian women they themselves are to be.

Paul speaks of the young women first encouraging them to listen to the older women and learn from them how to be godly wives and mothers.

So let us now look at what it is that the older women are to teach.

We find that there are seven instructions which are to be followed.

The first two go together. The younger women are to be trained to love their husbands and their children. The young Christian wife must have a serious attitude towards marriage and the home and must understand that love is the vital ingredient to a happy home. Hence, Paul puts it at the very beginning of his list of instructions which are to be taught.

Surely, you may be thinking, a young woman does not need to be taught to love her own husband and children. Perhaps we need to think again. Many marriages, including those of Christians, are in difficulty nowadays. Many children are not loved in the right way. Some mothers neglect their children; some are impatient, mean or abusive to them. Some children are showered with things but starved of time or love. Many are not disciplined. Some young mothers associate discipline and punishment with not loving their child. They want to be the child's friend, not its parent.

I heard of a nursery where the policy is now not to say "No!" to a child when she has misbehaved but to say, "No thank you!" And the staff there are now telling young mothers that it is not the child who has done wrong, (even though she clearly has) but the thing she has done is now what is seen to be wrong. In other words, they are doing away with sin in young human beings.

So we need to train young woman to think Biblically where child rearing is concerned so that they are not taken in by the current, modern methods and ways of thinking. They must be taught what the Bible says about wifely behaviour and godly discipline of children. This is vital for our society and our churches. We have a responsibility to teach the younger woman how to be successful wives, mothers and home makers.

All mothers can do with encouragement, support and help from time to time and this is an area where we can also help and be a source of blessing.

There may be some Christian young women who have non-Christian husbands. They will need particular care and oversight. The greatest priority in the home should be love. If a wife loves her husband and children according to the Biblical pattern, she is well on the way to making it a happy, secure marriage and home.

The third thing the young women are to be trained in is self-control. Self-control, one "variety" of the fruit of the Holy Spirit, is essential if we are to overcome temptation of any kind. If a woman cannot be self-controlled and discipline herself, how can she discipline her children?

But it is more than just that.

The word used for self-control here is the word that refers to the thought life of a person.

It is the same idea as where, in Timothy, Paul writes that God gave us a spirit of power, of love, of self-discipline and a sound mind. The meaning here is that a sensible outlook is what is needed. The church needs level-headed, self-controlled women just as much as self-controlled men. And this sensible outlook on life will filter down to sensible behaviour.

Fourthly, the younger women are to be trained to be pure. Paul has in mind married women in particular but much of what we are to teach will apply equally to single women. Paul insists on purity. The word in the Greek translated here as "to be pure" means "to be free from ceremonial defilement; to be holy; sacred; chaste; free from sin; innocent."

This righteous purity has two strands: outward chastity and inward purity of thought. The Christian wife must not fall into adultery or be unfaithful to her husband. Teaching sexual purity in our present-day culture is a huge challenge. God intended the sexual relationship between a husband and wife to be something wonderful and pure. Sadly, sinful human beings have perverted it to something dirty, sinful and wicked.

Married and single women must be taught by the older ones that this sexual purity is required by God. This purity commends the gospel to a fallen world, even though they may laugh and poke fun at the Christian who follows the Biblical way of life. When the Christian falls in this area of life, it is always seen as a scandal in the eyes of the world. It is a picture of the faithfulness of the church to Christ, her husband.

The requirement is also about her thoughts. So, what she watches on TV or reads in a magazine will affect her thinking. Paul includes the inward here. Her thoughts must be pure.

Our fifth and sixth instructions are to be busy at home, and to be kind.

The home is her priority. Her role here is seen as one of caring for the home and of managing the home well. This may sound old fashioned in today's culture and climate. But her home and family must come first before any career or activities outside the home.

A wife has a responsibility before God to ensure that her home is managed well. She must organise the home so that it is a place where her husband and children can thrive and be happy and fulfilled.

This is not a popular view today. But Biblical teaching, we must remind the younger women, is timeless. It doesn't change with the current ideas or the latest politically correct view which society holds.

Can a young wife do anything outside the home?

Scripture does seem to allow this. Proverbs 31 would suggest this is certainly the case, provided her priorities are Biblical and she is wise about her use of time and energy.

She is to be kind to those around her. We have looked at the need for Biblical discipline of children but this instruction to be kind must suggest that she does not rule her household with a rod of iron. No, she demonstrates firm, kind management and discipline.

She shows generosity to her family and to those outside. She will show compassion where needed and do kind deeds for those in need.

She will also open her home and show hospitality to those in need. This is an important way to show Christian kindness and can lead to opportunities to present the gospel.

And so we come to our seventh and final instruction. The young women are to be subject to their husbands.

No matter what our present culture says about women, if a wife is going to be in God's will she must be subject or submissive to her husband. This is the Biblical pattern for marriage, and we go against it as a society at our peril.

This position is much maligned and ridiculed today and so the Titus 2 woman must be particularly wise in teaching the young women what this does mean, and also, what it does not mean, in helping them to do what is Biblically right.

While the wife is busy running the home, the husband is still the leader, the head of the home. How unpopular this teaching is today. Feminist views have infiltrated the church and the views of many in the church.

I know of some young wives who in the early days of marriage have really struggled with this but their marriage has been blessed and their home has been a calm and peaceful place to raise their children, once this teaching has been accepted and they have chosen, with God's help, to be subject to their own husbands. But it must be taught! It does not come naturally to young women in our modern-day culture and society to submit in this way.

What is the ultimate reason for this? Why should wives submit to their husbands? Look back at the closing words of our passage: "so that no one will malign the word of God" [96]. They live in this way so that those outside the church will not malign the word of God.

What does this mean? They will not speak evil of it or show malice towards it or slander it in any way. Sadly, family problems cause unsaved people to sneer at the Bible and its teachings. So, the Christian wife's willingness to be submissive is for the gospel's sake, that those outside might see a difference in our godly Christian young women and be drawn themselves to the Saviour.

---

[96] Titus 2:5

You see, a godly woman is an advertisement for the gospel. Others will look on and see her contentment, her kindness and her submission and wonder at these things. The woman honours God's word when she lives by that word; she dishonours God and His word when she does not.

So, the bar is set high. The challenge is tough. This is a high calling to which we have been called and an awesome task that we older ladies have been given to do. But make no mistake about it, our society, our churches, and individual families will be radically changed for the better if we follow, with God's help, this Biblical pattern and glorious calling of womanhood to be the Titus 2 women He has designed us to be.

14

Angels

I wonder if you have noticed how increasingly the word 'angel' is being used in society? In particular, the word is used when speaking of the death of someone, particularly, though not exclusively, the death of a child or young person. The dead child or relative is now spoken of as being or having become an angel.

I read a newspaper article concerning a twenty-eight-year-old woman who had died a few weeks previously of cystic fibrosis. Towards the end of her life she had refused any further treatment. This was her goodbye message.

"I love you all, but I have decided to go, to be an angel so that I can watch over my beautiful loved ones instead."[97]

Another article showed a young woman whose sister had died from leukaemia. She had a tattoo inked on her back using ink and the ashes from her sister's cremation. The picture was that of her sister, now with wings as though an angel.[98]

Of course, we sympathise with those who have lost loved ones, particularly in tragic circumstances such as the loss of a child or a young person.

But we must not allow our sympathy and sorrow at people's loss and grief to cloud our thinking. We must not allow such worldly and erroneous thinking to permeate **our** thinking.

Some people even refer to their living children as their little angels. If we are Christians, we must guard against being carried along by the thinking of the world. Ultimately this will lead to us speaking as they

[97] https://www.independent.co.uk/news/uk/kirsty-bridges-28-year-old-beautician-decides-die-after-life-long-cystic-fibrosis-battle-a6791936.html accessed 6th April 2021

[98] https://www.mirror.co.uk/news/uk-news/grieving-woman-dead-sisters-ashes-7097282 accessed 6th April 2021

do. It is easy to become sentimental in our speaking and move away from what Scripture teaches. It is vital for the Christian to think Biblically.

To help us do that, we need to know what it is the Bible says about such heavenly beings.

What, then, do we know about angels? The Bible tells us a lot about angels. We sing of the angels in our carols at Christmas time, do we not?

But, are we convinced that such beings actually exist? We should be!

Why is that? Because the Bible speaks of there being angels and as Christians, we believe everything the Bible says is true.

The Bible tells us that angels are created beings. They were created by God.

What else can we learn about angels from the Bible? The Bible tells us that there are angels of darkness led by Satan.

In this chapter I want to focus on what we can learn of the role and purpose of good angels and be encouraged and helped as we move forward in our Christian life and walk.

There are about 300 different references in the Bible to angels. They show us that God has countless angels at His command, and He has commissioned them to help us as we live our life this side of eternity.

So, what then are angels?

They are created beings as has already been said. At one time there were no angels. Angels are among the invisible things made by God.

They are non-material. That is, they do not have physical bodies although they are known to take on a physical form when God appoints them to a particular task.

Angels are God's messengers whose chief job is to carry out His orders in the world. In fact, the word 'angel' simply means messenger so there's no surprise in recognising them in this role. God has given the angels higher knowledge, power and mobility than we have, so that they can assist Him in works of righteousness as He controls the universe.

What of their number?

The Bible speaks in terms of multitudes of angels, many thousands of thousands.

For example, Luke records this:

> *Suddenly a great company of the heavenly host appeared with the angel....*[99]

In Revelation John records what he sees:

> *Then I looked and heard the voice of many angels, numbering thousands upon thousands, and ten thousand times ten thousand.*[100]

Angels are mightier than men, but they are not gods. They cannot be in more than one place at any one time.

Christians must expect powerful angels to accompany them in their life experiences. They should not be surprised at this.

Demonic activity and Satan worship are on the increase in all parts of the world including our own land. The devil is alive and at work. The Bible tells us he realises his time is short but for the people of God, the devil's evil activities are counteracted by God's holy ministering angels.

We know from Psalm 91 that God has given His angels charge over us[101] so that with their help we can be victorious over Satan and the powers of darkness.

How can we be sure that there are angels active in the 21st century?

Are there really supernatural beings today that influence the affairs of human beings and nations?

We believe in angels because we believe in the truth of the Bible. But let's look at some real examples.

Let's begin by looking at the presence of angels in history.

The first time that angels are encountered in the Bible is in Genesis chapter 3.

Angels were placed at the gates of the Garden of Eden to seal the entrance and to ensure that Adam and Eve didn't return after their banishment by God. They were to guard the way to the tree of life.

Further on in the Old Testament, angels appear to Daniel.

---

[99] Luke 2:13
[100] Revelation 5:11
[101] Psalm 91:11 For He will command his angels concerning you to guard you in all your ways.

Daniel speaks to the king and says,

"..... My God sent his angel, and he shut the mouths of the lions. They have not hurt me, because I was found innocent in his sight. Nor have I ever done any wrong before you, O king."[102]

In the lions' den, Daniel knew the presence of the angel whose power was greater than the strength of the lions.

In the New Testament, in Matthew's Gospel, we read of the angel who rolled the stone away from the tomb of Jesus. He shone as a flash of lightening with dazzling brilliance. The guards at the tomb shook and became like dead men. As far as physical strength is concerned, the angel was infinitely stronger than any man and moved the huge stone singlehandedly, a weight several times more than a single man could move.

What, then, are some of the Biblical roles of angels?

These roles are under the instruction of God Himself. It is not an exhaustive list by any means. As we look at these roles, we will see examples of how angels have been working not just historically, but in more recent times and also in the 21st century.

1. Angels serve as guardians
2. Angels serve as messengers
3. Angels deliver us from harm, and they protect us
4. Angels minister to our needs
5. Angels tell us about the future
6. Angels worship God
7. Angels carry out the purposes of God

Let's consider three of these in greater detail.

Firstly, angels as **guardians**:

Many of us will have learned as a child that night-time prayer,

> Lord, keep us safe this night,
> secure from all our fears.
> May angels **guard** us while we sleep
> till morning light appears.[103]

---

[102] Daniel 6:22
[103] Attributed by some to Rev John Leland,1754-1841 – an American Baptist pastor from Massachusetts

The Lord Jehovah spoke to the people of Israel when they were in the wilderness making their way to the Promised Land.

God says,

> "See, I (that is, God) am sending an angel ahead of you to guard you along the way and to bring you to the place I have prepared. [104]

The psalmist declares in Psalm 91,

> For he (God) will command his angels concerning you
>   to guard you in all your ways;
> they will lift you up in their hands,
>   so that you will not strike your foot against a stone. [105]

Secondly, angels are God's **messengers.**

And what amazing messages they have delivered!

Angels proclaimed the birth of the baby Jesus at Bethlehem. Perhaps this was the greatest message of all.

An angel acting as God's messenger announced the resurrection of Christ.

God uses angels, as well as men of course, to declare the message of salvation, the good news of the saving work of Christ at Calvary.

In the letter to the Hebrews we read,

> Are not all angels ministering spirits sent to serve those who will inherit salvation? [106]

What a wonderful honour it will be for angels to know us by name and share our rejoicing over those who come to saving faith in Christ.

In Acts chapter 8 [107] Philip the deacon received instructions from God brought by an angel to go to the desert where he met the Ethiopian to whom he preached the Gospel.

Angels appeared to John in his isolation on the Isle of Patmos with God's message which forms what we know as the book of Revelation concerning the end of time.

Thirdly, angels **protect** us and deliver us from harm.

The most important characteristic of angels is not that they have power to exercise control over our lives, but that they work on our

---

[104] Exodus 23:20
[105] Psalm 91:11-12
[106] Hebrews 1:14
[107] Acts 8:26

behalf. They are motivated by an unmoving love for God and a desire to see His will fulfilled in us.

Every Christian should be encouraged, strengthened and thankful knowing that angels are watching over us. We should always be grateful for the goodness of God, who uses such wonderful friends called angels to protect us and care for us according to His bidding.

We see again in the psalms, this time in Psalm 34, that angels protect and deliver us from harm.

We read,

> *The angel of the LORD encamps around those who fear him –*
> *that is, God,*
> *and he delivers them.*[108]

A few other Biblical examples of such angelic delivery include an angel of God travelling with the Israelites and delivering them from the grip of tyranny in Egypt recorded in the book of Numbers;[109] Daniel's delivery from the lion's den;[110] and Peter's delivery from prison[111] in the New Testament.

So far, we have looked at some of the appearances of angels in the Bible.

But there are modern day examples of the work of angels, for it is important to realise that their role in serving God continues up to the present day and ongoing into the future as the Lord wills.

The Reverend John G Paton, a missionary in the New Hebrides Islands, tells a thrilling story involving the protective care of angels. Hostile natives surrounded his mission headquarters one night, intent on burning it down and killing the Patons. John Paton and his wife prayed all night, a night filled with utter terror, that God would deliver them. When daylight came, they were amazed to see their attackers leave. They gave thanks to God for delivering them.

A year or so later, the chief of the local tribe became a Christian! Mr Paton asked the chief what had stopped him and his men from burning down the house and killing them, on that night some months before.

---

[108] Psalm 34:7
[109] Numbers 20:16
[110] Daniel 6:22
[111] Acts 12:7

The chief looked surprised and replied, "Who were all those men you had with you there?"

The missionary replied, "There were no men there, only my wife and me."

The chief disagreed. He said they had seen many men standing guard. He said there had been hundreds of men in shining garments with drawn swords in their hands. He said they seemed to circle the mission station so that the natives were afraid to attack. Only then did Mr Paton realise that God had sent His angels to protect him and his wife.

Billy Graham's father-in-law, Dr Bell, served as a physician in China. He bought Christian books and tracts from a Christian bookshop in Shanghai to give to his patients at the hospital. He relates an incident which occurred in 1942 after the Japanese had won the war with China.

One morning a Japanese truck stopped outside the bookshop. It was half filled with books. The Chinese Christian shop assistant realised with alarm that the Japanese had come to seize the books from this shop as they had done from many other bookshops in the city.

Just as the five Japanese marines were about to enter, a well-dressed Chinese gentleman entered the store, a complete stranger to the shop assistant.

For some unknown reason, the marines didn't enter the shop but looked through the windows. For two hours they loitered outside the shop but didn't enter. The stranger asked the shop assistant what they wanted and then he prayed with the assistant and encouraged him to do the same. This was how they passed the two hours.

Finally, the marines jumped back into their truck and drove away. The stranger then left without explaining who he was and without making any purchases. Might this stranger have been one of God's protecting angels?

A final example of angels' protection comes from the story of Corrie Ten Boom, of whom many of you will have heard.

She writes of a remarkable experience in the appalling Nazi Ravensbrück prison camp. These are Corrie's own words,

> I took her arm, and together we entered the terrifying building. At a table were women who took away all our

possessions. Everyone had to undress completely and then go to a room where her hair was checked.

I asked a woman who was busy checking the possessions of the new arrivals if I might use the toilet. She pointed to a door, and I discovered that the convenience was nothing more than a hole in the shower room floor. Betsie, (Corrie's sister) stayed close beside me all the time. Suddenly I had an inspiration.

'Quick, take off your woollen underwear', I whispered to her. I rolled it up with mine and laid the bundle in a corner with my little Bible. The spot was alive with cockroaches, but I didn't worry about that. I felt wonderfully relieved and happy.

'The Lord is busy answering our prayers, Betsie', I whispered. 'We shall not have to make the sacrifice of all our clothes'.

We hurried back to the row of women waiting to be undressed. A little later, after we had had our showers and put on our shirts and shabby dresses, I hid the roll of underwear and my Bible under my dress.

It did bulge out obviously through my dress. But I prayed, 'Lord, cause now your angels to surround me and let them not be transparent today for the guards must not see me'.

I felt perfectly at ease. Calmly I passed the guards. Everyone was checked, from the front, the sides and the back. Not a bulge escaped the eyes of the guards. The woman just in front of me had hidden a woollen vest under her dress. It was taken from her. But they let me pass for they did not see me!! Whereas Betsie, right behind me, was searched.

But outside there was further danger. On each side of the door were women who looked everyone over a second time. They felt over the body of each one who passed. I knew they would not see me for the angels were still surrounding me. I was not even surprised when they passed me by but within me rose the jubilant cry, 'O Lord, if you so answer prayer, I can face even Ravensbrück unafraid.' [112]

How utterly amazing and humbling!

It would be amiss of me to finish this chapter about angels without reference to the book of Hebrews, where we see clearly that Christ is far superior to them. It is through Christ and His redemptive work at Calvary that we have salvation and our relationship with a holy God is restored. It is not through the angels. Here are some verses to illustrate the point – they are all from the first chapter of Hebrews:

For to which of the angels did God ever say,
"You are my Son;
>*today I have become your Father"?*
>*Or again,*
"I will be his Father,
>*and he will be my Son"?[113]*
And again, when God brings his firstborn into the world, he says,
"Let all God's angels worship him."
>*In speaking of the angels he says,*
"He makes his angels winds,
>*his servants flames of fire."*
>*But about the Son he says,*
"Your throne, O God, will last for ever and ever,
>*and righteousness will be the sceptre of your kingdom.[114]*

A little later in the chapter a rhetorical question is asked:

To which of the angels did God ever say,
>*"Sit at my right hand*
until I make your enemies
>*a footstool for your feet"?[115]*

---

[112] Quoted in *Angels – God's Secret Agents*, Billy Graham, Hodder Christian Paperbacks, 1975, p88-89. The original text is found in *A Prisoner And Yet ...*, Corrie ten Boom, first published in 1954. A substantial part of the book is available free in Google Books. It is from chapter 4 *The Horrors of Ravensbrück – Angels Round About Us* which does appear in the Google Books version.
[113] Hebrews 1:5
[114] Hebrews 1:8
[115] Hebrews 1:13

And finally:

> *Are not all angels ministering spirits sent to serve those who will inherit salvation?*[116]

Who are those who will inherit salvation? They are the ones brought into the kingdom of God by the atoning work of Christ. That includes you and me if we are Christ's and have come to Him in faith. The angels **serve**. Christ **saves**. This is a hugely important distinction which needs to be made.

There's a lot more we could say and learn about angels. I hope your appetite has been whetted to find out more about angels from the Bible and trust that you have been encouraged and strengthened in your faith by some of the things you have read about.

And next time you hear someone refer to a human being as 'my little angel', perhaps you can use that as an opportunity to tell them simply what an angel actually is, and then tell them of the One who created not only the angels but is their Creator and the One who came to earth to be their Saviour.

[116] Hebrews 1:14

15

Facing trials

As long as the Christian remains in this world, she will be under pressure of one kind or another.

James begins his letter in the first chapter by telling his readers to face the facts of life. It is not **if** they face trials but **when** they face trials.

It is the same for us living in the 21ˢᵗ century. And when such trials and suffering come our way, (and come our way, they surely will for all of us at some time or another), it causes us to re-examine the Bible to see what God is teaching us there about our response to such things.

How do we cope as Christians when we are faced with problems and difficulties which we may feel are at times too much for us to bear? What does the Bible have to say to us when we feel totally overwhelmed by something which has happened to us?

In this chapter, I want us to look at some verses from the epistle of James, which will help us to answer these questions.

James' letter is very practical. He helps us to look at our trials from a Christian point of view, or perspective if you will. Having a living personal faith in the Lord Jesus Christ makes all the difference in the world when we come to cope with whatever our sufferings might be. This faith is an active faith. It enables us to overcome the difficulties in our life and to be victorious.

Here is the real test of our faith, not when all is well but when things are hard to bear. For all of us it is easier to praise God and recognise His goodness when life is going along smoothly, and it seems as though God is blessing us in many ways.

But how strong is our faith in times of testing and trial? For our faith will inevitably be put to the test in the hard experiences of life. Then there seems to be an apparent contradiction between what we are experiencing in our daily life, and the promises we read, of God's blessing. We may ask the questions "why?", or "does God still love me?", or "what have I done to deserve this suffering?"

We must remember that trials are sent by God in order to make a person stronger in their faith and closer to God Himself in their Christian walk.

In testing us, God is aiming at our development, to improve our character and help us grow as Christians.

Perhaps what we find in the letter of James might come as a surprise to some people reading this book.

For we find that the first words James writes in his letter after his greeting are these:

> *Consider it pure joy, my brothers, whenever you face trials of many kinds...*[117]

Pure joy? Did I read that correctly, you may be thinking? Surely this is the last thing we would expect to do! The whole idea seems absurd.

You could very well understand a response to those words, to quote a well-known tennis player, as being:

"James, you cannot be serious!"[118]

Or "James, you are joking, I presume."

It may be one thing to see trials as testing our faith and endurance as a Christian, but quite another to regard them with joy! This kind of statement is mind boggling and it certainly grabs our attention. We might say we are blown away by such a command as this.

These words were not just some glib theory spoken to James' audience. No, he knew that as converted Jews they knew what it was to suffer. They would have experienced racial prejudice; they were a despised minority. For his audience, to stand up for Christ was a costly business. Yet James is calling on his readers to count their suffering as pure joy, not just something to put up with.

When we look into the New Testament, we find many examples of Christians who express their sheer joy in moments of severest trials.

Let's look at a few examples.

---

[117] James 1:2
[118] John McEnroe, Wimbledon championships, 22nd June, 1981

When the apostles were flogged for preaching the gospel, we are told that

> *The apostles left the Sanhedrin, rejoicing because they had been counted worthy of suffering disgrace for the Name.*[119]

When Paul and Silas were flogged and jailed at Philippi, we are told that even in the middle of the night they were praying and singing hymns to God.[120]

Paul writes to the church in Corinth that

> *in all our troubles my joy knows no bounds*[121]

and later in the same letter he tells his readers,

> *I delight in weaknesses, in insults, in hardships, in persecutions and in difficulties.*[122]

How is it possible for these people to rejoice in such circumstances? How can James tell us to do the same?

What exactly is James teaching here?

He is saying that anything that casts us down or sets us back, anything that makes us angry or resentful, anything that is said to us or done to us- all that is included in the word trials- we must count as "pure joy".

In our natural state we will always tend to ask why a trial is happening to us. What did I do wrong? When will this ever end?

We will naturally feel frustrated, angry and in despair. But if we adopt the attitude in life that James speaks of, then our troubles and difficulties will not rob us of our joy.

What James is telling us is that as an act of faith we must see our trials as a positive gain and not as something negative.

This does not mean that we will not experience pain and distress. Of course, we will.

Nor does it mean going about with an artificial smile on our face. It does mean that suffering can be turned into joy through believing faith in the Lord Jesus Christ. Our suffering can be used by the Lord to draw us into a closer relationship with Him.

---

[119] Acts 5:41
[120] Acts 16:25
[121] 2 Corinthians 7:4
[122] 2 Corinthians 12:10

James shows us that there is a reason why the Christian should rejoice when faced with difficulties in her life, and we'll come to that in a moment.

This at first seems a bitter pill to swallow. How, we may ask, can we turn such trials and tribulations into blessings? This does not seem possible. Nor on the face of it does it seem comprehensible. We cannot understand how these things can be. Yet it is abundantly clear from Scripture that we are not required to understand such things but are required to obey God's word. We must have a "no matter what" attitude to obedience.

The writer to the Hebrews tells us,

> No discipline seems pleasant at the time, but painful. Later on, however, it produces a harvest of righteousness and peace for those who have been trained by it. [123]

To help us understand this, let us consider for a moment the example of a sportsman. We know how he must train and how much sweat and tears will no doubt be produced before he reaches his goal and is successful in his chosen sport.

So it is, in the Christian life for all who profess to be followers of Christ. For us to grow and develop in our spiritual life, including counting our trials as joy, we must apply the same principle as the one training to be a great sportsman or sportswoman. And just as it has to be an act of discipline and will for the sportsman to persevere through the pain and failures in order to achieve his goal, so it is with the believer. It requires an act of will on her part, through faith in the Lord Jesus Christ to bring joy out of the suffering experienced in the Christian life.

For what is the alternative left to us?

We can wallow in self-pity and feel sorry for ourselves; we can dwell on what might have been if things had turned out differently. We can allow ourselves to become hard and bitter, to become resentful perhaps towards others and even towards God Himself because of what has happened to us. If we do this, we do the devil's work for him.

---

[123] Hebrews 12:11

For the Christian there is another way and God calls us to choose to deal with our trials His way, through trusting in the Lord Jesus Christ.

What are the reasons then for making trials "pure joy"? Why should we rejoice?

James answers this question for us:

> Consider it pure joy, my brothers, whenever you face trials of many kinds, [3] because you know that the testing of your faith develops perseverance. [4] Perseverance must finish its work so that you may be mature and complete, not lacking anything.[124]

First of all, he talks about perseverance. If we go back to our analogy of the sportsman once more, we will better understand perseverance. It is that willingness to keep going, that determination to finish the race despite aching limbs and a bursting chest. When everything we are feeling tells us to give up, we push on as hard as we can for the prize at the end of the race. If this is how it is in a race in sport, then how much more in the race of life, - the Christian life?

For when there is true faith in the heart, testing actually produces perseverance in the believer as she looks towards the final goal.

Paul wrote the following to the church in Rome:

> ..... we also rejoice in our sufferings, because we know that suffering produces perseverance; perseverance, character; and character, hope.[125]

There we have it again. Joy in suffering.

But you know, wonderful as this is, there is more to it than that.

In our weakness we find true strength in Christ; in our great need we discover the abundance of God's grace supplying all our needs. In times of darkness, the living faith of the Christian shines through as never before, and all of this has come about because we have endured trials and testing.

The same thread can be seen in Psalm 119.

> Before I was afflicted I went astray,
> but now I obey your word.[126]

---

[124] James 1:2-4
[125] Romans 5:3-4
[126] Psalm 119:67

Suffering and affliction are tools used by God in His wisdom, to keep us from straying from Himself. How marvellous is that!

Now perhaps we begin to see a glimpse of the joy that James is speaking of.

So, far from diminishing our faith or causing us to lose it, or turning us away from the Lord, the hard path we tread in life actually serves to draw us closer to Him with a deeper commitment than ever before.

We pray more in our greater need and ultimately grow in personal holiness. Now that is something to be joyful about, is it not?

James gives us further reasons for counting trials as pure joy.

> *Perseverance must finish its work so that you may be mature and complete, not lacking anything.*[127]

The key words here are "mature" and "complete". The job, if you like, of perseverance is to enable the Christian to grow in godliness and to be sanctified as we make our journey through this life towards the next. The goal is shown here to be maturity and completeness however hard that journey may be. There is no giving up, no turning back where God is concerned, for He will carry on the work He has begun in the life of the believer and see it through to completion.

In his letter to the church in Philippi the apostle Paul writes,

> *In all my prayers for all of you, I always pray with joy* [5] *because of your partnership in the gospel from the first day until now,* [6] *being confident of this, that he who began a good work in you will carry it on to completion until the day of Christ Jesus.*[128]

Perseverance must finish its work, writes James. What work is he speaking of? It is the work of developing our Christian character through persevering which must go on until God's purpose for our life is complete.

It might be helpful to think of it in these terms. Certain elements of holy character can only grow in the soil of trouble and must be watered by our tears.

---

[127] James 1:4
[128] Philippians 1:4-6

So here we can sum up what is being said in these verses in the sequence that is set out in Scripture.

The Biblical sequence is this:

➢ trials
➢ pure joy
➢ perseverance
➢ maturity
➢ completion

I wonder, if we were putting these in order, where would we have put pure joy? Might it not have been at the end of the list?

In other words, our sequence might have looked like this

➢ trials
➢ perseverance
➢ maturity
➢ completion
➢ pure joy

Might we not expect joy to be ours after we have persevered and reached our goal? It seems reasonable, wouldn't you say?

But the Lord, through James, is telling us otherwise.

For although we do have joy in knowing our final reward is in heaven, yet we are to exhibit joy here and now, during our daily life, for it is that joy that enables us to persevere.

So, getting things in the right order in the sequence, in a Biblical order, is essential for our spiritual growth and well-being.

Finally, what an encouragement it is for us when we find James writing:

> *Blessed is the man who perseveres under trial, because when he has stood the test, he will receive the crown of life that God has promised to those who love him.*[129]

In this verse we see that those who persevere during trials in this way are described as being "blessed". The tense is present, not future.

*"Blessed **is** the man"*

For the Christian, who perseveres in her faith during trials and difficulties, there will be blessing from God as she goes through suffering and sorrow.

---

[129] James 1:12

But the Christian does not suffer as the non-Christian person suffers.

Let me explain what I mean by that.

When the non-Christian suffers, she might put up with it, she may grin and bear it, and she may steel herself to get through.

But she will not endure as the Christian does. For we learn in this verse that Christian joy is not just about the future but is a present experience for believers, as they go through trials and difficulties.

Can you see here the outworking of what James wrote in the second verse, the verse which was our starting point?

As we, in obedience, *"consider it pure joy whenever we face trials of many kinds"*, so we receive God's blessing in those very trials. How amazing! And how encouraging for us if we can but grasp these wonderful truths.

You see, there is a crown of life ahead for those of us who are believers. Once again, if we think of the example we used earlier of the sportsman, there is of course only one winner in a sports race. But in the Christian race of life, all believers are winners!

Hebrews chapter 12 speaks about persevering in the Christian life.

> *Therefore, since we are surrounded by such a great cloud of witnesses, let us throw off everything that hinders and the sin that so easily entangles, and let us run with perseverance the race marked out for us.*[130]

The athlete runs in suitable running clothes and is not weighed down with heavy clothing or bags. The Christian must do the same and when the finishing line is approached, those who have gone before will be cheering her on, and the Lord Himself will be at the finishing wire to welcome His child.

Then those of us who are Christians will receive the crown of life, the ultimate reward for the Christian in heaven, where we will reign with Christ and all of His people for evermore.

Who is this promise for? It is for those who love Christ. Many will know suffering, hardship, sorrow, trials, anguish, devastation, and these things come to the believer and the unbeliever alike.

---

[130] Hebrews 12:1

But only those who know these things **and** love the Lord will share in everlasting life and receive the reward at the end of the race.

So, if you as yet do not know the Lord as your personal Saviour, can I implore you to consider these things with great urgency and come to Him today while there is still time?

And may we who are His followers be encouraged, no matter what our trials and difficulties may be, to persevere to the end of the race and share in that ultimate and wonderful prize which is heaven itself.

16

Cheer Up!

We all need a word of encouragement! I want to give you a word of encouragement - literally a word.

It comes from the New Testament. The word in the original Greek is θαρσέω or, more simply understood, *tharseo*. It is a verb which is always used as a command and is found in only six different contexts.

It can be translated in various ways, as meaning "take courage", "take heart" or "cheer up".

Let's look at the six times this word appears in Scripture and be encouraged.

1. You have been called

In Mark chapter 10, we read of poor blind Bartimaeus, sitting begging by the roadside as Jesus leaves the city of Jericho.

He shouts out, *Jesus, Son of David, have mercy on me.*[131]

Many try to silence him, but he shouts out even more. Then, to the astonishment of the crowd, Jesus stops and says, "*Call him.*"

So, they call to Bartimaeus,

Cheer up! On your feet! He's calling you.

If you are a Christian, perhaps you remember calling out for Jesus to show you mercy, only to discover that He was actually calling you.

Then, like Bartimaeus, you came to faith. You received your spiritual sight and followed Jesus along life's path.

If you want reasons to be cheerful and to feel encouraged, surely this is a good place to start.

It is good to remember, if you are a Christian, how you first received grace and mercy in hearing the gospel and were enabled to respond to Christ's call.

[131] Mark 10:47 and 48

2. You have been forgiven

In Matthew chapter 9 we have the account of the paralysed man who was let down through a roof by his friends, right in front of Jesus.

Seeing the faith of the man's friends, Jesus says,

Take heart, son, your sins are forgiven.[132]

We know how the Lord Jesus went on to heal the man's paralysis as a demonstration of His divine power and authority to the unbelieving teachers of the law.

The sense of being forgiven, even at the human level, is one of the sweetest and most comforting of blessings. Yet others can forgive us only for the wrongs we have committed against them. So, the leaders of the law were right when they stressed that man's sins could be forgiven by only God because ultimately all our sin is against Him.

How then can Christians be discouraged and miserable for long if they have truly experienced the forgiveness of God?

Surely this is another reason to be encouraged and cheerful.

3. You have been saved

Continuing in chapter 9 of Matthew's Gospel, we again have Matthew's account, the shortest one, of a famous incident and once more he adds this word of encouragement which we are considering.

Jesus is on His way to raise from the dead the young child of a synagogue leader.

A woman who had had a health matter to deal with for twelve years, one which would have meant she was excluded from any synagogue, somehow manages to force her way through the throngs of people and touches the edge of Jesus' cloak.

More detail of the same story is given in Mark's Gospel chapter 5, where we read that Jesus senses that healing power has gone out of Him. Everything comes to a standstill when He asks who has touched Him.

The woman is anxious about what she has done. She comes forward and kneels at the feet of Jesus, telling Him her story.

Back in the story recorded by Matthew, Jesus replies,

[132] Matthew 9:2

Take heart, daughter, your faith has healed you.[133]

The Saviour is compassionate. He has a special place in His heart for the poor, the weak, the fearful and those who are side-lined by society.

Our word of encouragement in this story brings peace and joy to all Christians who find themselves in such a situation where they are in need of Jesus' special touch upon their life.

For if you have put your trust in Jesus you are indeed saved! The woman was healed from her ongoing medical condition, but the believer is saved from her sins and has everlasting life in Him.

If you have not as yet taken that step of faith, then come to Him today. He will welcome you with open arms and then you too will be encouraged and full of joy and cheerfulness.

4. You have Jesus with you

This time we turn to Mark chapter 6.

Following the feeding of the 5000, Jesus sends His disciples ahead of Him in a boat and goes up a mountain to pray.

As night approached, Jesus saw that the disciples were straining at the oars to row the boat against the wind.

Shortly before dawn, Jesus walked on the water towards them. The disciples, thinking they had seen a ghost, were very frightened and cried out in terror.

Straightaway, Jesus spoke to them and said,

Take courage! It is I. Don't be afraid.[134]

Then He climbed into the boat with them and the wind died down.

Once again, the disciples are being taught by Jesus how they should respond.

Previously when they had been afraid on the water, Jesus had been with them and had stilled the storm, but this time things were very different. Since Jesus didn't go with them from the outset, the disciples must have thought they had to rely on themselves and deal with the rising wind on their own. Perhaps they felt that Jesus had left

---

[133] Matthew 9:22
[134] Mark 6:50

149

them to their own devices and was no longer there to help them. They might have been very perplexed at His apparent abandonment.

Sometimes, we might feel like that. We can feel alone, as though God is far from us, perhaps even that He doesn't really care about the difficulties and troubles we are going through and have to cope with.

And yet, all night long Jesus had been watching and praying for His disciples from the mountain top.

So it is for us. If we are one of His children, we know the Lord is watching over us and will never leave us or forsake us. His word says so! We may not always feel it, but we believe it by faith.

And what is more, He will never test us beyond our strength. He will eventually come to us, often in ways that surprise us.

When He speaks that word of encouragement, "take courage" we can know for certain that it is the Lord and He is with us.

5. You will continue to go on serving the Lord

Our Biblical reference point for our fifth use of the word under consideration is taken from Acts chapter 23 verse 11.

It had been a challenging and difficult few days for the apostle Paul in Jerusalem. Three times Paul had needed to be rescued by the Roman forces from the growing anger of the Jews, twice from the crowds in the temple and also from the Sanhedrin itself.

Paul, a Roman citizen, wanted to be allowed to go to Rome. But as he slept at night, away from the anger and violence of the crowds in the Roman barracks, he may have been wondering if his work of serving the Lord was at an end. There was so much more he wanted to do but it seems as though the Lord was shutting the door. We read that the following night the Lord stood near Paul and said,

> Take courage! As you have testified about me in Jerusalem, so you must also testify in Rome.[135]

What further confirmation could Paul want or need, that there was still work for him to do in God's kingdom? The Lord Himself was speaking to him!

Paul's vision and intension for the future had always been to take the word of God to Rome and now he had this amazing confirmation

---

[135] Acts 23:11

from heaven itself that not only was his ministry to continue but would do so in Rome itself.

Have you ever felt that your days of productive service for the Lord might be over? Particularly as we get older, it is easy to feel like that, is it not?

Once again, no matter what our circumstances may be, we must **take courage**. We must not allow ourselves to become despondent and feel a sense of uselessness in our Christian service. We must be encouraged to know that, while the Lord allows us to continue our earthly pilgrimage, He will always have work for us to do. Ask God to open up opportunities for serving. He is faithful and will not let you down.

It is important to use our God given gifts, whatever they may be, in the work of the kingdom. And, even when we perhaps find that age and infirmity prevent us doing those things we did in our younger days, we must not forget the power of prayer. The older Christian who is a prayer warrior, who underpins the work of the church and those serving in it, is herself serving in such a vital way.

6.   You have entered into Christ's victory

In John's Gospel, we read Jesus' final words in the upper room before His great high priestly prayer.

The disciples finally begin to understand who Jesus is, where He has come from and where He is going. Their earlier despondency when they realised that He is going to be taken from them lessens. Jesus warns them that there will be trouble ahead which they will have to face and in the light of that, He encourages them with these concluding words,

> *"I have told you these things, so that in me you may have peace. In this world you will have trouble. But take heart! I have overcome the world."*[136]

Here is the ultimate word of encouragement. This world is full of trouble and fears for the faithful Christian. *But*, says Jesus. And what an important "but" that is. Stop and think about it for moment.

---

[136] John 16:33

Despite all that the Christian has to face in this world, we can be encouraged when we remember that Jesus has conquered the world and with it, death. As a result, if we are His followers, we have entered into that victory. We are still in the world, yet we are also in Christ, and that means, says Jesus, we have peace. That peace is God-given and cannot be taken from us. It is a peace in our heart that passes all understanding. It is a peace that the world looks at with bewilderment.

What can be more encouraging than that?

What can give us more cause for joy and cheerfulness, despite our circumstances, than that?

Thus far, we have been told what we should be. We should be cheerful and take heart, and we have seen a number of reasons to encourage us to do just that.

But what about the other side of the picture, if you like? What is it we are told **not** to be?

I want us to consider just one passage to help us further.

In the first chapter of the book of Joshua, we are given a commandment by God. First of all, the positive, which is to be strong and courageous, and then the Lord says to Joshua,

> "...... *Do not be terrified; do not be discouraged, for the* LORD *your God will be with you wherever you go.* "[137]

Moses was now dead. The Israelites were bereft. From a human perspective, we can well understand them being fearful as they look to an uncertain future without him.

He was their great leader, the one who, under the guiding and leading hand of God Himself, had led them out of Egypt and delivered them from the tyranny and oppression of the Egyptians.

He was the one who had brought them the ten commandments, having met with God on Mount Sinai.

He was the one who had been with them through the many years of wandering in the desert, bringing them almost to the point of entering the promised land.

It must have seemed a daunting situation to find themselves in, facing the next chapter of their national history without him.

---

[137] Joshua 1:9

How would they ever do that and enter the land God had promised them without Moses' leadership?

How would they face the enemies that were before them in Canaan itself?

They would have to take on those people who had lived in the land for very many years and who would not easily give up their land, certainly not without a fight.

We can understand their fearfulness and deep concerns that they would have been feeling as we are so often afraid when faced with new and difficult circumstances.

At least, their fear is understandable when looked at from a human perspective.

But that is when God is left out of the picture. It was important for the people of Israel and also for us to remember that leaders like Moses come and go. They are at best human beings. Death is part of the cycle of life. Ministers in the church also come and go.

The One who is constant, the One who does not come and go or indeed change in any way is God Himself.

So, we need to look at Joshua chapter 1 from God's perspective.

Moses was undoubtedly a great leader. He is among that great list of men and women of faith recorded for us in Hebrews chapter 11.

Nevertheless, there is a warning here not to become too dependent on leaders in the church or in any other sphere of life. We must not rely on them totally. It is true that God does give such people to the church in the role of pastors, teachers, evangelists and so on. And we are, of course, grateful for that but ultimately, we are to put our trust in Christ and be totally dependent on Him, the unchanging One, not on a man. God is the constant, not a man.

God is a God who keeps His promises. He has already promised the land to the people, therefore, why should they now be afraid? They can know for certain that God will keep His promises and give them the land.

Another reason for not being afraid is that no enemy or army will be able to stand against Joshua or defeat him and his forces since the Lord is with him, as He was with Moses before him.

Deuteronomy chapter 7 clearly shows how their victory is assured as the Lord promises to be with them in fighting their enemies.

In the first chapter of Joshua, the Lord tells Joshua to be strong and courageous.

> *"Be strong and courageous, because you will lead these people to inherit the land I swore to their forefathers to give them.*
>
> *Be strong and very courageous. Be careful to obey all the law my servant Moses gave you; do not turn from it to the right or to the left, that you may be successful wherever you go.*[138]
>
> *Have I not commanded you? Be strong and courageous. Do not be terrified; do not be discouraged, for the LORD your God will be with you wherever you go."*[139]

They are to go out to fight, being brave and showing their strength in the Lord who has promised to be with them. They are to show an active faith, not one which is passive.

God equips them to go into battle without being afraid. There are three ways in which God provides for them, so they are able to do so with courage and strength.

Firstly, He promises to be with them.

Secondly, He raises up a new leader to replace Moses and promises to be with him, Joshua, as He had been with Moses.

Thirdly, the people have God's word which they are told to meditate on day and night. This will be a lamp to their feet and a light to their path.

How relevant and pertinent these three provisions are for us today, for the church and those of us who are part of it.

The Lord continues to promise to never leave us and He has given us His Holy Spirit to dwell within us and be our Helper.

He gives leaders, overseers, to shepherd the flock and to teach them Biblical truths so that they are able to fight the good fight, to stand against the wiles of the Devil and the attacks of the world around them.

We also have His word, the Bible, which is the same today as it has always been.

---

[138] Joshua 1:6-7
[139] Joshua 1:9

As Paul writes to the young Timothy:

All Scripture is God-breathed and is useful for teaching, rebuking, correcting and training in righteousness, so that the man of God may be thoroughly equipped for every good work.[140]

God's people are not to be afraid or discouraged. We are still called on today to be strong and courageous in what we have to face as we follow the Lord in faith and obedience.

If you are a non-Christian reading this book, it is important to stress once again that, in your present state before God, all that has been said thus far concerning courage and cheerfulness does not apply to you.

But it soon can!

If you will turn to the Lord Jesus Christ in repentance and faith and accept Him into your life as your own Saviour and Lord, then you too will know the joy of having sins forgiven and peace with God.

So, we come back to where we began – back to that little Greek word θαρσέω – *tharseo*.

You who are believers in the Lord Jesus Christ, **take courage, take heart and cheer up!**

---

[140] 2 Timothy 3:16-17

17

Let Justice Prevail[141]

Our first point asks the question: What is justice?

Justice, according to the dictionary, is the administering of deserved punishment; it is when the punishment fits the crime.

I'm sure we all have our ideas about justice. We all want justice to be done and to be seen to be done, do we not? We read items in our newspapers every day and hold up our hands in disbelief, and say where is the justice in this or that? We might ask what has happened to British justice. It seems so often nowadays the punishment most certainly does not fit the crime. We equate justice with fairness, do we not?

Our second point considers justice in the Bible

Let justice prevail.

So, whose justice exactly is it that we want to prevail? To prevail is to succeed, to win out or to dominate.

As we so often see, what one person, what one judge even, sees as just may be very different from another.

To answer this question, we must turn to the Bible, to God's holy book; this is our reference point for how we should live. This book is cast aside by most people today as being out of date, old fashioned, boring and irrelevant. Most homes do not have a copy or if they do it is confined to a bookshelf to gather dust. But none of these things about the Bible is true. God's word is for all generations, for all time and is as relevant today for us in 21st century Britain as when it was first written many years ago.

---

[141] This chapter along with the next two chapters are based on talks given on three separate occasions at services organised by a local constituency of the Women's World Day of Prayer. The theme and a certain amount of material were prescribed for me – the gospel emphasis is that of the writer.

The question of justice is found right through the Bible, in both the Old and New Testaments. So, we can be certain that God is very much concerned about justice. In fact, Scripture records that God is angry about the injustices He sees in the world and therefore, it must follow that we too should be concerned about justice. We should do whatever we can to improve things in our country and throughout the world where we see injustices occurring. It is right for those of us who are Christians to act as salt and light in an otherwise dark world.

So, let us return to justice in the Bible.

In Exodus chapter 20, God gave the people of Israel the 10 commandments, you may remember, and He then, in Exodus 23 gives them laws of justice and mercy. Many verses are to be found in the Old Testament calling for justice to be administered according to these God given laws.

As has already been said, so often we see many injustices in our land today as well as throughout the world. This is not a new problem.

It was a problem which the prophet Habakkuk found some 600 years before the birth of Christ. The book of Habakkuk explores the question of whether God permits evil to exist without being punished and if so, why. Today, we see the wicked apparently flourishing and we may ask questions about God's justice in these things.

We will find God's answer in the little book of Habakkuk. God shows His justice by always keeping His word and fulfilling what He promises. He always vindicates His own people. This is the whole message of the book of Habakkuk.

Let's look at the context for a moment. Josiah was king. He was a godly king.

During his reign there was a time of revival, albeit short lived, when the Temple was restored, and the Feast of the Passover was reinstituted in the land. Yet, Habakkuk was deeply troubled by events of his day and, following the death of Josiah, the nation quickly returned to its evil ways.

Habakkuk, like Job, questions God's justice. but in the end, both of them are brought to realise that God is Sovereign, and His justice is far beyond their comprehension.

God's justice demands that wickedness be punished, wherever that wickedness is found, among pagan nations or His own people. The

158

book of Habakkuk is organised as a dialogue between the prophet and God. Unusually for a prophet, he does not speak to the people of God directly.

Habakkuk saw the decline of the nation, both morally and spiritually.

Isn't this something we see in our own nation today?

Habakkuk has to learn to rely totally on the wisdom and justice of God even when he does not understand what God is doing. And by the end of the book, he is no longer complaining against God but is full of praise and worship.

You see, he was struggling to understand the purposes of God, something I'm sure many of us struggle with. But in the dialogue that he has, God's words are words of reassurance that He is in control, just as they are for us today.

Chapters 1 and 2 take us through Habakkuk's two complaints and God's answers.

First of all, Habakkuk is disappointed that God does not seem to be answering his prayers. He believes God is letting sin go unpunished and therefore there is no justice in the land. God appears to be tolerating sin and Habakkuk believes God's inactivity, as he sees it, has made injustice worse.

The rich use their power and money to get what they want. The poor are oppressed, and their rights are trampled on. The righteous who remain in the land find life hard because as they seek to obey God's law they are held back.

Does this sound familiar? He could be writing these exact same words about Britain today!

But then God answers him.

At the beginning of chapter 1 we read that God uses the nations to bring about His own purposes. He controls the political scene. In fact, He uses some wicked nations to punish other wicked nations. Habakkuk asks how God can possibly allow His own people to suffer as they were and be punished and destroyed by the heathen, sinful Babylonians. How could God do this sort of thing?

Habakkuk was facing the age-old dilemma which many of us still face today. Why does evil seem to go unpunished? Habakkuk was asking why God did not step in and end the plans of the wicked Babylonians.

How can a righteous God tolerate such things?

Then we have God's response.

God is just and merciful, even though His people do not understand His ways. God tells Habakkuk that everything will be alright, but he must not look at the immediate, at the present. No, he must take the long-term view and he will find that God will show His righteousness and justice. The people of Israel deserved punishment at that time. God was using the Babylonians temporarily; later on, they too would know God's justice for they themselves would be destroyed. God is absolutely just. Wickedness will eventually be punished, and the righteous will ultimately see God's justice.

God assures Habakkuk that He will punish all the wicked at the right time. In other words, judgment will come upon the wicked in His time, in God's time which is always perfect. For God is neither too early nor too late in bringing about any of His plans when dealing with human beings. And we can be certain of these two things - the final destruction of evil, which includes all injustice, and the triumph of God.

What does this mean for those of us who are Christians?

The key phrase here is *the righteous will live by his faith*.[142]

A proud, puffed up person relies on himself whereas the righteous person, the Christian, the one who has put her faith in Christ, relies on God. It will take faith to wait patiently for God's plan to unfold.

God's suffering people are called to have faith and to believe that God's purposes for the world and for His people will prevail. This faith is an ongoing trust in God and in His promises even when things are dark and difficult in our life. The righteous person must go on believing that God's promises are true, and He will bring about His plans and purposes.

Let's consider further the statement that *the righteous will live by his faith*.

---

[142] Habakkuk 2:4

There are two possible ways of life; what we might call the way of reason and the way of faith. In other words, there are only two possible attitudes to life in this world, that of faith or unbelief.

The righteous, the verse tells us, shall live by faith; the woman who lives by faith is righteous. Whatever we do with our lives is based either on faith or unbelief. We either take the word of God and live by it or we do not.

The Biblical way, the way for the Christian, is living by faith. What does this mean in practice? It means believing what God says just because He says it; and more than that, it means basing the whole of our life upon faith in God and His word.

Is there anyone reading this who is still putting their confidence in this world and what it has to offer? What is controlling your life? Is it the wisdom of this world or is it the word of God? Each one must answer for herself in the quietness of her own heart.

The Bible tells us that what really matters is the coming of God's kingdom, for this life and this world are only transient. Is your life based on faith? Do you read the Bible and believe that what you read there is true, living your life accordingly?

As Habakkuk came to realise, the wicked may seem to triumph and justice may seem **not** to be prevailing, for a while, but this is not how things will continue to be in the longer term.

Why does God allow this to be the case?

He allows it for His own purposes and to fulfil His own plans for the whole of eternity. The world may stagger along under evil powers, lawlessness and injustice, before God Himself, in His own time, shows Himself in mighty power and brings great glory to His own name.

Thus, we come to Habakkuk's prayer in chapter 3.

Habakkuk has heard of the great saving acts of God. In his prayer, he pleads with God, the great judge of the earth to show mercy to the wicked.

Anticipating great destruction at the hands of the Babylonians, we see a great change in Habakkuk.

He began back in chapter 1 by telling God how to run His world; he ends in chapter 3 by trusting in God to bring about justice in a way that only He knows best.

As Abraham said on one occasion when speaking to the Lord:

Will not the Judge of all the earth do right?[143]

Abraham knew that His God could do no other; now Habakkuk had at last learnt the same. Despite suffering and loss, Habakkuk has learnt that he can trust God and with that trust comes great joy, not in his circumstances but in God Himself. The Lord God is now the prophet's strength. Habakkuk's feet are now steady and sure. His confidence in God will carry him through whatever his circumstances and situation may be.

Our third point considers justice and the Gospel

We have already seen that God is a just God, who will one day bring all His plans to fruition and triumph over all evil. This is a joyous and reassuring message for those concerned about justice and the lack of justice we see in the world today.

It is though also a solemn thought which brings with it a warning.

Paul, in assessing the state of humanity, writes in his letter to the Romans, quoting from the Psalms:

There is no one righteous, not even one; there is no one who understands, no one who seeks God. All have turned away, they have together become worthless; there is no one who does good, not even one.[144]

These words are also found in Psalm 14, in Psalm 53 and in Ecclesiastes 7.

So now we are faced with a dilemma. The Bible clearly states that not one righteous or just man or woman is to be found, and yet at the same time we know we all have to one day stand before a holy, righteous and just God.

For His justice to prevail, therefore, there must be punishment for all; for every human being who ever lived. There is no other way. A just and righteous God, the God of the Bible of whom we have been

---

[143] Genesis 18:25
[144] Romans 3:10-12 – being a quotation from Psalm 14:1-3; Psalm 53:1-3 and also Ecclesiastes 7:20

thinking, in order to be true to Himself and to who He is, must punish sin. For sin is an abomination to God.

How awful if the message were to stop there. But this same God, this God of justice is a God of love, of grace and mercy. Before the beginning of time as we know it, in the heavenly places, God put together a wonderful, amazing rescue plan.

This was a plan of salvation which satisfied both sides of the nature of God, as it were. It was a plan whereby justice was done by seeing that sin was punished yet restoring sinners to a living and eternal relationship with God, which had been broken back in Genesis and the Garden of Eden.

It was a plan of perfect justice.

For God sent His only Son, the Lord Jesus Christ from the splendour of heaven to this world of ours. He came as God in human form, He Himself being fully God and the only One who was perfect and sinless.

He was crucified on the cross of Calvary, something we remember particularly at Easter time. This death did not come about because of some plan devised by the Jewish Pharisees and priests of the day who hated Jesus. No, not at all. This plan of salvation was set in motion by God the Father with the full knowledge and cooperation of Jesus Himself.

And whilst He hung there and suffered on that cross, He who had committed no sin took the punishment for us, who had. How awesome is this! If you are a Christian reading this, your heart will surely be thrilled as once again you hear the old, old story of what Christ has done for you.

John chapter 15 reminds us of what an amazing act of sacrifice this was when it says,

> Greater love has no one than this, that he lay down his life for his friends.[145]

The American pastor John MacArthur sums it up in such a helpful and moving way, like this:

> On the cross God treated Christ
> as if He had lived my life of sin

---

[145] John 15:13

So that He could treat me
as if I had lived Christ's life of righteousness.[146]

This is truly amazing!

We know that Jesus rose again on Easter Sunday. Death and the grave could not hold Him. He was victorious over death, sin and Satan, and by His death and resurrection, we, who should come under the punishment of God the Father as justice is put in place, are no longer condemned or under judgment.

If we are trusting in Jesus and are seeking to follow Him in our life day by day, then we have the righteousness of Christ placed like a robe on our shoulders. The penalty for our sin has already been paid. Our sins have been forgiven.

We read in 1 John chapter 1,

*If we confess our sins, He is faithful and **just** to forgive us our sins and to cleanse us from all unrighteousness.*[147]

Here the justice of God comes in again and we see that by His justice God forgives us. It was His justice coupled with His love and mercy that provided the way for our forgiveness.

If you are not a Christian, may I speak directly to you?

Do you want to see justice prevail?

Then you need to come to Jesus and come to Him now while there is still time.

Call on Him to forgive your sins. Give your heart and life over to the One who, in order that God's justice might be done, gave up the splendour of heaven and gave His life on Calvary for you.

You need to be covered by the righteousness of Christ before that fearful and awful final day when He will return in all glory and honour and power as the Victorious One.

All of us must do all we can to right the wrongs that we see in our land and indeed in the world around us as we are able.

---

[146] Quoted from a summary of John MacArthur's message *Fifteen Words of Hope* to be found at https://www.gty.org/library/Print/Blog/B160826 accessed June 30th 2021

[147] 1 John 1:9

But above all, we need the courage to go forth and tell those we meet about the God with whom one day we will all have to do, and whose justice will finally prevail.

18

How many loaves have you?

This chapter will challenge you to consider the gifts you have and to think about how you can share what you have with others.

The Bible passage in 1 Kings chapter 17 shows us the ultimate in sacrificial giving. Here we have a poor nameless widow who only has enough food for one meal for herself and her son. She shares what she has with Elijah, a foreigner and a stranger. She puts her trust in God to provide for her needs after listening to the words of Elijah.

It is not enough to be aware of the needs of others. We must do what we can to meet those needs and share what we have. Jesus wants us to act; to be doers of the word not just hearers.

Let us take a moment to look at what sort of needs these may be and how we might seek to address them.

First of all, there are physical needs: need of food, clean water to drink, basic clothing for warmth, medical supplies and somewhere to live. It is an absolute scandal that we in the western world waste so much food, while there are many thousands of people in other parts of the world who are starving and do not know where the next meal is coming from.

Did you know that around half of all fruit and vegetables grown by our farmers is rejected by the supermarkets and is destroyed? Why? Not because it is rotten or infected in some way but because it is the wrong shape or size to satisfy the British consumer. We must examine our own hearts in this matter. On average, each person in this country throws away enough good food to save 2 people from starvation. Do we fall into the commercial trap of slavishly following "best by dates" and "use by dates"? We must examine our own actions before God and if we are at fault, seek to put things right.

In what ways can we help meet these physical needs?

We can offer financial support.

In the country of Chile, the work of Father Alberto Hurtado[148] is well known. In the first half of the 20th century, he sought to help in practical ways the underprivileged, the outcasts of society by founding what came to be known as "Christ's Homes" – *Hogar de Cristo*.[149] In these homes, vulnerable people were fed on home baked bread and were provided with a warming hot drink. How was this work funded? Fund raising campaigns were organised under the heading "Give until it hurts".

What a challenge this is to us. Do we know anything at all of this kind of giving? Do we give at all? Do we perhaps give the minimum? Or do we give in such a sacrificial way that it hurts? These are challenging questions for us all to consider.

The Bible tell us in 2 Corinthians chapter 9 that God loves a cheerful giver.[150] If we give faithfully to the work of God's kingdom, He will bless us and honour us for our obedience.

I have found that there is what I would describe as a chain effect when we give to others. What do I mean by this? As Christians, we do not give in order to get back, as so many in the world might do. No, not at all.

When we give to those in need, they themselves can give to others who are more in need. In this way many are blessed including the giver.

In what other ways can we help meet these needs?

We can support in prayer.

This is a very important work. We may not be able to go to somewhere like Chile to help in a practical way. But we can pray for those in need, for the hungry and homeless and we can pray for those working amongst such communities to bring them relief.

Think for a moment about the story of the feeding of the 5000, found in the 6th chapter of Mark's gospel. Jesus and His disciples are sensitive to and aware of the people's need for food.

When the disciples suggest sending them away to buy food, Jesus asks

---

[148] https://en.wikipedia.org/wiki/Alberto_Hurtado accessed 6th April 2021
[149] https://en.wikipedia.org/wiki/Hogar_de_Cristo accessed 6th April 2021
[150] 2 Corinthians 9:7

Have many loaves have you?[151]

We know what happens next. We see the miracle of feeding 5000 people with 5 loaves and 2 fish, not to mention 12 baskets of left-over food.

Jesus calls on us today to share what we have, just as the boy did in this story and from our sharing much blessing will come.

Jesus is the same today as He was in Bible times. He is with us in our churches. Our gifts, given to Jesus in whatever way He calls, will multiply as the loaves and fish did.

There are a number of other passages in Scripture where we see God providing for His people.

God feeds His people manna in the wilderness, you remember. In 2 Kings[152] we read of Elisha feeding 100 men from 20 loaves of barley bread and some ears of new corn, and there was even some left over!

The needs of our world challenge us but they are not insurmountable, nor need they overwhelm us if they are done in Christ's name and in His strength.

We have considered so far the physical needs of the poor. Now we must look at their spiritual needs.

If we give bread to the poor without giving them the Bread of Life, that is, telling them of the saving work of the Lord Jesus Christ, then we do them a tremendous disservice and are not serving the Lord as we should. There are other agencies which are able to carry out humanitarian relief work, but for the Christian, that is not enough.

Conversely, we cannot preach the Gospel to those who are starving and lacking in basic human needs without showing God's love and care for them in doing all we can to meet their material needs.

This is why it is so important to support Christian relief organisations, charities and missionaries who, under God's leading, seek to do both of these things.

We may have been focusing our thoughts on the needs of people in far off lands.

But the people in your own country, in your own town, in your own neighbourhood have similar needs too. They have physical

[151] Mark 6:38, also Mark 8:5 and 15:34
[152] 2 Kings 4:42-44

needs. They have emotional needs and they most certainly have spiritual needs.

If you are a Christian, God has placed you in this harvest field. He wants you to share what you have with the poor and needy of this world, but also to remember those closer to home whom you may meet on a daily basis. He may be asking you to show compassion to those you meet or to open your home to someone who is lonely.

We are each called to share the love of Christ and the good news of the gospel to those who are otherwise going to a lost eternity.

May you take up this challenge in obedience to your Heavenly Father and know His rich blessing as you do so.

19

Streams in the Desert

"Streams in the desert. "

This phrase almost suggests a contradiction, doesn't it? For when we think of a desert, we do not routinely think of a stream. Try to picture in your mind's eye a desert. These descriptions may help you.

A desert is a place that is dry, barren, arid, a wasteland, a wilderness with no water; a place of drought, treeless and usually sandy. It is an area where few forms of life can exist because of lack of water; a region so arid because of little rainfall that it can support little or no vegetation. It is a land uncultivated and largely uninhabited. It is lifeless.

A traveller wrote of a visit to Dubai when he was taken on a ride across the desert in a 4-wheel drive vehicle. There was not a stream in sight. Not even a puddle. There was gritty sand and scrub and that was it.

It is said that where there are streams in the desert, they are related to sudden torrential rain and flash flooding. Such is the awesome power unleashed during these storms that roads and bridges can be swept away.

But this rainfall also brings life. Some of the most glorious pictures that have ever been seen show the Australian outback in bloom where it has rained after 20 or more years of drought. [153]

So, when we think about streams in the desert, what do they do?

They transform it completely, don't they? Think of a stream in a parched and barren land. We can now picture life, hope, growth - an oasis.

The Bible speaks of streams in the desert.

---

[153] https://www.abc.net.au/news/2016-10-24/outback-wildflowers-full-bloom-winter-rain/7958980 accessed 6th April 2021

"Streams in the desert, the promise of a future."

We read in Isaiah chapter 35,

The desert and the parched land will be glad;
the wilderness will rejoice and blossom.
Like the crocus, ² it will burst into bloom;
it will rejoice greatly and shout for joy.
The glory of Lebanon will be given to it,
the splendour of Carmel and Sharon;
they will see the glory of the LORD,
the splendour of our God. .....[154]
Then will the lame leap like a deer,
and the mute tongue shout for joy.
Water will gush forth in the wilderness
and streams in the desert.[155]

From the dark picture of judgment in the earlier chapters of the prophecy, Isaiah turns now to the light of God's salvation. He is using concrete imagery here to depict the refreshment which Jesus, the Water of Life, will bring to a spiritual waste land.

The prophet Isaiah is pointing forward to the promise of a future where the desert will blossom, the streams will flow and there will be great rejoicing.

He is thinking of times of spiritual barrenness, spiritual desolation. Isaiah paints the future for us in pictures. A day is coming when the wilderness will be transformed into a fruitful field; when the desert will blossom with the crocus, the first flower of spring; when the dry places will be turned into springs of water; when the earth will be transformed into a Garden of Eden, the paradise we read of in Genesis. In other words, the whole world as we know it is to be changed.

You see, the wilderness will no longer be a wilderness.

How is this possible, you ask? Well of course, it is the Lord Himself who will bring about these changes. Scripture tells us that all of nature looks eagerly towards the return of the Lord Jesus. Then there will be no more parched ground, no more thirsty ground because

---

[154] Isaiah 35:1-2
[155] Isaiah 35:6

the land will be changed and will be like a glorious garden. There will be streams in the desert on the earth when Christ returns one day!

Isaiah uses this promise of the coming of the kingdom to bring strength to those who are weak or afraid both in his time and to us in our day. This glimpse which we are given of the new heavens and the new earth is to encourage us in our Christian walk.

Verses 5 and 6 refer to the work of divine salvation. God's saving work will make His people new. They will have a new life, a new birth. The renewal of life in nature illustrates for us what has happened to those of us who are saved. Only God can bring about this transformation in nature, bringing water and streams in the desert, and pools and springs to the thirsty ground.

And only God can bring about this transformation in us.

"Streams in the desert of the church"

Staying with Isaiah, in chapter 44, we have the promise of revival:

> *"But now listen, O Jacob, my servant,*
> *Israel, whom I have chosen.*
> *This is what the LORD says—*
> *he who made you, who formed you in the womb,*
> *and who will help you:*
> *Do not be afraid, O Jacob, my servant,*
> *Jeshurun, whom I have chosen.*
> *For I will pour water on the thirsty land,*
> *and streams on the dry ground;*
> *I will pour out my Spirit on your offspring,*
> *and my blessing on your descendants.*
> *They will spring up like grass in a meadow,*
> *like poplar trees by flowing streams.*
> *One will say, 'I belong to the LORD';*
> *another will call himself by the name of Jacob;*
> *still another will write on his hand, 'The LORD's',*
> *and will take the name Israel.*[156]

---

[156] Isaiah 44:1-5

Promises like this are to be found throughout Isaiah's prophecy.

Relieving thirst is the Bible's way of describing the experience of God's blessings. The blessing Isaiah now speaks of is the revival of God's church from its current stagnant condition. God reveals in Scripture and throughout church history that He intends to advance His church through revival.

A few things can be said about revival:

➢ Revival follows a period of spiritual barrenness and desolation.
➢ Revival is a sovereign work of God
➢ When God comes in revival to renew His church it is accompanied by a conviction of sin of those already in the church.
➢ Revival is a work of the Holy Spirit

And so it is, that we see the streams in the desert in the church when revival comes.

We need the courage and the faith to pray for these kinds of blessings to come to the spiritual drought that we see in our land, and in our churches today.

"Streams in the desert, offered to every individual"

We come now to the very personal application of our subject, the transformation that takes place in **us.**

We read in John chapter 4 the story of the woman at the well. The Samaritan woman was a moral outcast because of the way she lived. That's the very reason why she came to draw water from the well at midday. No one in their right mind would ordinarily do that. The heat would be overwhelming! The townswomen would have come either in the early morning or in the cool of the evening to get water.

This woman needed to avoid the other women, their stares, their gossip, their hostility. She was rejected by them because of her sin. But Jesus spoke to her against all the conventions of the day. Remember it is clear from what He says to her that He knew all about her. He offers her living water.

Jesus answered her, "If you knew the gift of God and who it is that asks you for a drink, you would have asked him and he would have given you living water."[157]

At first the woman doesn't understand what Jesus is talking about. When she first meets Him, she is aware of nothing more about Him than that He is a thirsty Jew. Like all sinners, she is blind to Christ, and is more interested in the things of this life than about the things of eternity and the life to come.

There is something here for each one of us to consider. She no doubt thought Jesus was offering her some strange new water which, if she drank it, would quench her physical thirst for good.

But as the story unfolds, it becomes clear that Jesus is talking not about physical water, but about what He called "living water", the water of life, that eternally satisfying life which only God Himself can give.

The woman does not understand this. She takes this to mean literal physical water. She displays another trait of the non-Christian, to confuse the physical with the spiritual. Jesus points out to her that the things of the world do not satisfy. Those who drink from Jacob's well or any other source of physical water will get thirsty again as we all do, but those who drink of the living water offered by Christ will never thirst.

In other words, without Christ, men and women will always "thirst again". Jesus promises that the water of life He speaks of will spring up in the heart and will be a constant source of refreshment and satisfaction. Once again, the woman does not understand. She asks for this water so that she doesn't have to visit the well again with all the problems that entails.

Perhaps, given the society we live in and the amount of rain we have in our country, it is difficult for us to grasp just how vital water was, and still is, in Middle Eastern society. If you couldn't get sufficient water, your crops wouldn't grow, your cattle and flocks would die of thirst: you and your family would not survive.

Water really was and is life sustaining. So a constant supply of water was essential and was life giving in a very real way. For this

---

[157] John 4:10

woman to be offered a supply of water, which would never fail or dry up, would be seen as the greatest of all blessings.

But Jesus was telling the Samaritan woman that He was not offering her physical literal water, but He was able to give her the joy, peace, satisfaction, acceptance and meaning to her life which deep down she needed and really longed for.

The problem was, you see, she was looking for satisfaction in the wrong place. Like so many people, then and today, she had rejected the source of true satisfaction, the spring of living water, God Himself.

I wonder, is there a reader who is like that? You may be someone who is trying to do things your own way and that is bound to lead to failure. That is what we do if we try to live our lives in our own way, not God's way. We fail. We find no peace, and nothing will satisfy the longings of our soul.

I said a moment ago that those who drink of the living water will never thirst again.

What does it mean, to "never thirst"? Does the Christian believer never feel discontent or dissatisfied? No! It means that Christ satisfies the human desire for a relationship with God in the here and now, and for the promise of eternal life.

Let me try to make this clearer. We sometimes say that it is as if there is a hole inside each one of us. It has been put there by God. It is shaped like God, if you like. Only God can fill the hole. Only God can satisfy our inner thirst.

People try many things to satisfy this desire. They turn to drugs, drink, parties, money and so on. And often with tragic consequences. They don't know where to go to find satisfaction. We see suicides on the rise, do we not? When in despair people seek death as a way out of their situation.

Further on in the passage in John's gospel, Jesus shows the woman that the important thing is not religion but knowing God the Father in a real and personal way. For her and for those of us living in the 21st century, that can only be done when we have our sins forgiven and know salvation through the death and resurrection of Christ Himself.

Jesus has now shown the woman her sins, her desire for satisfaction and the emptiness of life without Christ. We see that the woman's eyes are finally opened by the Saviour; she puts her trust in Him and is saved.

But what about you, dear reader? Remember, Jesus knows everything about each one of us. He knows your need. He knows your heart. Do you know what it is to drink of this living water? Do you know the Lord Jesus as your personal Saviour? Have you repented of your sins and asked Him into your life?

If you have not turned to the Saviour, can I urge you to do so? He will not fail you. And you will know those streams of living water in that desert of your own soul, both now and for all eternity.

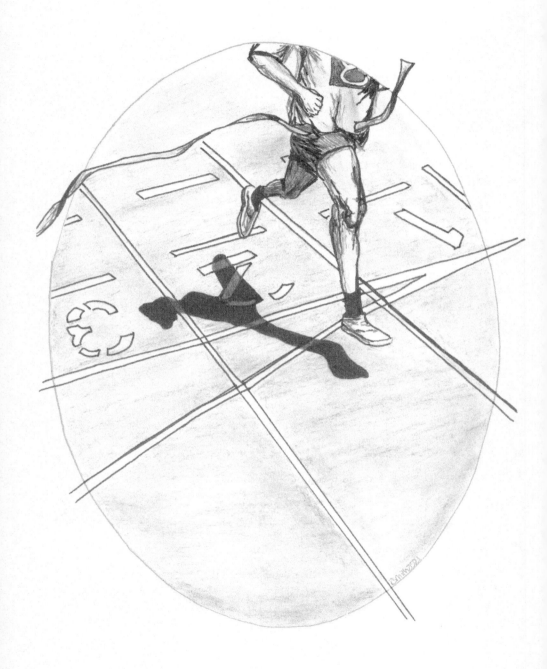

20

Finishing well

Life for the Christian believer is a journey which proceeds through enemy territory. For those of us who are believers, that course in life is lined with trials and tribulations and many of us will testify to the fact that at times our pilgrimage is exhausting. That journey is made more trying and difficult because of our own weakness and inward conflict. But it is the only way to reach the city of God. This journey leads ultimately to the rest and the inheritance we are promised in Christ.

Our spiritual progress as we make this journey of life requires discipline, training, focus, and effort much like running a race.

There are a number of places in the Bible where the writer, generally Paul, likens the Christian life to a race. For example:

> *I have fought the good fight, I have finished the race, I have kept the faith. Now there is in store for me the crown of righteousness, which the Lord, the righteous Judge, will award to me on that day—and not only to me, but also to all who have longed for his appearing.*[158]

On another occasion he writes:

> *Brothers, I do not consider myself yet to have taken hold of it. But one thing I do: Forgetting what is behind and straining towards what is ahead, I press on towards the goal to win the prize for which God has called me heavenwards in Christ Jesus.*[159]

Now, I don't know how many of you can run a race. Running about in the park with my grandchildren is about as much as I can manage these days!

[158] 2 Timothy 4:7-8
[159] Philippians 3:13-14

Nevertheless, I **am** going to ask the question "Are you running to win the race, the race of faith?" Of course, I am now speaking spiritually and not literally.

Paul in these verses is painting a picture for us, of running a race and moving towards a final goal. In reading the Bible, we discover that there is no age limit in this race. There is no retirement from running in this spiritual race. We must keep on running until we reach the final goal.

In particular, the words of Hebrews chapter 12 will help us to run the race successfully and help us to finish our earthly pilgrimage well. Here the writer uses the phrase "Let us" three times in verses 1 and 2.

We are called on to be involved in three distinct actions.

1.   to run the race
2.   to lay aside everything that hinders us in that race
3.   to look to Jesus.

I want to unpack each of these in turn and see how as we age and face new challenges, we can be encouraged to keep on going despite the hardships we may have to face. Action is needed on the part of the Christian believer. We are not to be passive. We do not believe in an "everything in the garden is rosy" kind of Gospel. No, that is wrong and not what Scripture teaches.

People fall away when problems come along for this very reason. They have been told that if they come to Christ, they will have wealth, health and nothing will go wrong for them. Nothing could be further from the truth. Christ said if we follow Him, we will share in His sufferings and will know persecution and trials as He did.

The main theme of our passage is endurance or patience. The Jewish believers who received this letter were getting weary and wanted to give up. The writer encourages them to keep on moving forward in their Christian lives like runners running in a race. I hope that all of us who are believers, who are citizens of the kingdom of God will be encouraged through God's word to do the same.

So, what does Hebrews chapter 12 tell us about how to run the race?

The first "let us" says,

Let us *throw off everything that hinders and the sin that so easily entangles.*[160]

The picture the writer has here in his mind is of athletes striving for victory before a crowd of spectators. He may have been thinking about the Greek "footrace" so called, a test of fitness and endurance. This footrace was one of the five contests of the pentathlon in the great Olympic Games, and always came first. It was the only athletic contest that lasted for an extended period. The athlete had to discipline himself to discard everything that might hinder him as he ran the race. Anything that would impede progress is left behind. Only light clothes must be worn and there must be no excess baggage.

Apparently, athletes used to wear heavy training weights to help them in their preparation for the races. No athlete would ever dream of actually competing while wearing these weights as they would slow him down and would hinder rather than help him win the race. In fact, at that time, they ran naked – the men and women having their races on different occasions!

So, it is for the Christian, running the Christian race. The Christian is to remove all weights (not her clothes, though!) from her life which would hinder and impede progress on her earthly journey to her heavenly home.

What then are these weights that we as Christians should remove to enable us to win the race?

The verse tells us everything that hinders our progress is to be thrown off. They may even be "good things" in the eyes of others. There may be nothing wrong with them in and of themselves but if they are a hindrance and are slowing us down then they must still be cast aside. You see, things that hinder us are not necessarily sinful but can still be those things which hinder our individual Christian progress.

Let me give you some examples to make this as clear as possible. Perhaps it is the love of money that is a weight for some one. Or it might be our desire to be approved of by others so that being popular in the eyes of other people becomes more important than pleasing

---

[160] Hebrews 12:1

Christ. This may then cause us to stumble as we run the race towards our goal.

Maybe for a younger person ambition to attain or achieve this world's goals distracts them from following Christ.

Or is it how we use our time? Perhaps we enjoy reading novels, or gardening or playing golf. If these kinds of seemingly good pursuits become more important than serving Christ, then they can be described as weights.

Do we put worldly pursuits before prayer and Bible study, or attendance at the services on Sunday and in the week? If so, then whatever it is, it has to go. We are told to seek first the kingdom of God and His righteousness, and all our needs will be taken care of by God Himself. Each one of us must examine our own heart and throw off those things which are coming between us and God.

But we also need to look at the other side of the coin, for the writer goes on to instruct the readers to throw off the sin that so easily entangles.

It is important to realise that we are in a battle, in a war. We struggle against sin. We must strive against it. Otherwise, just like the weights we have been speaking of, it also will hold us back. Before we know where we are, we have been tripped up and hurled to the ground in a race which, at the outset, had all the possibilities of a triumphant victory.

We can compare these sins to a loose garment which ends up around the limbs of a runner, entangling her and slowing her down, and ultimately preventing her finishing the race. We don't want to be tripped up at the end of the race. We want to finish the race well.

What then does the writer have in mind here and how is it different from the weights?

Firstly, it will be any sin that prevents us reaching our goal. We as Christians must strive to avoid any particular sin which we know will entangle us and pull us down. That may be different things for different believers. But in particular for all believers, is the sin of unbelief. Under pressure, these Hebrew Christians doubted their faith and wanted to return to their old way of life which was seen as easier. Easier perhaps in the short term but in the long term they would not finish the race if they turned back in unbelief. And it is the same for us today. We must guard against unbelief and lack of faith and say to the Lord, "I believe. Help me with my unbelief."

Even after regeneration, believers retain their old sinful nature, what the Bible calls "the flesh" alongside the new nature we have in Christ.

To run effectively, then, we must be active in throwing off both the weights and sin. We must put off the "old man" and put on the new by faith in an ongoing process. The weights of this life are never far away, and we are never free from indwelling sin. We have a lifetime's work therefore in mortifying the flesh and denying its ungodly desires. This battle never ends until we get to glory. The victory, the attaining of the prize, can only be won by faith in Christ, not by willpower but in Christ alone.

Now we come to the second "let us" which answers the question, "How are we to run?"

> Let us run with perseverance the race that is marked out for us.[161]

Christian believers must run with perseverance.

In the Christian race, there are no prizes for those who do not persevere to the end of the course. I looked up the word "perseverance" in the dictionary. It defined perseverance as a steady persistence in a course of action.

A second meaning of perseverance is continuing in a state of grace to the end until death comes. It is an activity maintained in spite of difficulties. The idea here is of endurance, of not giving up. Those of us who follow Christ can expect to share in His sufferings and must expect to experience opposition from those around us who are outside of Christ, as well as expect rejection, pain, tribulation and trials. But in the face of all these things we are called upon to run with perseverance, to endure to the end and to not give up.

Notice that the race is marked out for us. We don't make our own track or decide our own route.

We have been called by God to be a participant in this race and we follow the path He has set out for us. Our ultimate goal is of course heaven.

---

[161] Hebrews 12:1b

The athlete, say, at the Olympics has her eye on the ultimate prize for her, the gold medal. That is not the prize the Christian is seeking. No, for the Christian the ultimate prize is not a perishable token of greatness but an imperishable crown! A crown of glory. If we run well the race marked out for us, we will attain this tremendous prize, a crown of glory.

How is this possible, you ask?

Encouraging witnesses and present contestants in the race with us to encourage us, along with the promised reward of heaven, our ultimate goal, will not ultimately bring us to the end of the race. We must look to Christ and Him alone.

So, this brings us to our third and final "let us":

Let us fix our eyes upon Jesus....[162]

This verse tells us **where we must look**.

In the course of the race, the eyes of every Christian athlete must be directed firmly and continually at the Lord Jesus Himself. This is an action that we who are in this spiritual race must determine in our own lives to do. It is the action of one who deliberately looks away from other things and fixes their eyes on Christ constantly during the whole struggle, knowing Christ is always near.

One of our grandchildren was born visually impaired. Something he always found difficult when running in the school sports day illustrates this point very well. While he looked ahead, he could run reasonably well but as soon as another runner came alongside him and began to overtake him, he stopped looking ahead; he stopped fixing his eyes on the finishing line and looked at the other runner. This slowed him down and he inevitably failed to win the race.

The writer encourages us to fix our eyes on Jesus as our goal, and in doing so, our faith and our hope will be strengthened.

You see, Christ has already run the race of faith and has conquered for us. The verse goes on to say He is the author and perfecter of our faith. What He starts He finishes, in order to see us through to victory and to the finishing line!

[162] Hebrews 12:2

The Lord Jesus went through many trials when here on earth. His battle against sin took Him to the cross with all the shame and suffering involved.

We are told that He is the one that we are to consider:

> *Consider him who endured such opposition from sinful men, so that you will not grow weary and lose heart.*[163]

Consider this same Jesus. Look to Him. Look to Him when the race gets difficult as it surely will.

Do you remember that children's song we used to sing?

> *When the road is rough and steep,*
> *Fix your eyes upon Jesus.*
> *He alone has power to keep.*
> *Fix your eyes upon Him.*[164]

It's not just for children, is it? Here in a children's song is a profound and Biblical truth for us all whatever our age.

This then is how we cope. This is how we keep going to the end of the race of faith. We get our encouragement and our strength from Christ. We need to take our eyes away from ourselves, away from other people, away from our circumstances and problems and fix them upon the Lord Jesus Christ and Him alone. This is the open secret of Christian perseverance. The strength to run the race and complete it comes only by looking to Christ.

Having humbled Himself to die on the cross for our salvation, God the Father now exalts Christ to this special place; a place of supremacy, a place of honour, a place of privilege, a place of power and glory.

And, if we are among those redeemed by Christ, then one day, we too will share in this our reward in heaven. It will be ours as long as we endure to the end. This was no time for the Christians in the letter to the Hebrews to turn back. And it is no time for us to give up either, whatever we have to face in this earthly life.

Why should you consider Jesus? So that you will not grow weary and lose heart.

---

[163] Hebrews 12:3

[164] Norman J Clayton, © 1985 Norman Clayton Publishing, administered by CopyCare Ltd. See Junior Praise Combined, #279.

Old age is no time to turn back or give up the race whatever sufferings we have to face. Earthly trials actually testify to the fatherly discipline of God and teach us to be more reliant on God. They are meant to teach us endurance rather than to cause us to give up.

So, throw off your weights and sins, run with perseverance, and look to Jesus! Then if we live to old age, we will reach our goal. Our Heavenly Father will take us to be with Him one day and we will know eternity in the presence of the Lord Jesus where we can praise and worship Him forever.

God preserves His people when they are buffeted by Satan, making His strength perfect in their weakness and proving His grace is sufficient for them. He preserves them with a watchful eye, a powerful arm and a loving heart. See how He has kept you thus far. Look to Him and trust Him to preserve you until your journey's end. You will not be disappointed!

If anyone who has read this book would like to know more about the Christian faith and the gospel, please contact the author at *fel.enquiries@outlook.com*

Printed in Great Britain
by Amazon